I0525441

TALES AND ESSAYS FROM
OLD JAPAN

TALES and ESSAYS
FROM
Old Japan

LAFCADIO HEARN

Introduction by Edwin McClellan

GREEN
POINT
BOOKS

This Greenpoint Books edition is a reprint of the work
originally published in 1956 by Gateway Editions.

All rights reserved:
No part of this book may be reproduced or transmitted,
in any form or by any means, without permission

For information, address:
Greenpoint Books, Ltd.
767 South 4th Street
Philadelphia, PA 19147
info@greenpointbooks.com

Paper: 979-8-88677-032-2
Cloth: 979-8-88677-033-9

Cover design
by Michael Schrauzer

INTRODUCTION

Lafcadio Hearn died fifty-one years ago, and at the time of his death much of what he loved in Japan was fast disappearing; for Japan, in order to survive as an independent nation, had been forced to adopt the ways of an alien civilization which were harsher and uglier, though more efficient, than her own.

Black Ships, and the great industrial power that they represented, had forced open the door to Japan so that Westerners might come in and trade. And Japan, in order to escape the indignity already suffered by the other countries of the East, began to modernize herself; and modernization, for her, meant that a feudal society, which had gone on for hundreds of years without change, had to be transformed into an efficient industrial state.

Such a transformation, which had already begun when Hearn went to Japan in 1890, he knew to be necessary, if she was to keep her independence. But he regretted the necessity profoundly, because he saw that with the change would come ugliness, the kind of ugliness which is inevitable in an industrial society, and which he had come to know too well in twenty years of wandering. Unlike many of his fellow Westerners, who praised Japan because she was imitating the West so successfully, Hearn loved Japan because, despite the revolution and despite Western influences, there was still left in that country much that was old and beautiful, and much that a man of his temperament and inclinations could admire. The ancient castle towns, the Buddhist and Shinto temples, the courteous peasants, priests and gentry,—these he loved and admired, and hoped that they would never be entirely replaced by cities of concrete, factories, industrial workers, and civil servants.

Hearn's attachment to old Japan arose from a deep conservatism in his character, not from an indiscriminate fondness for the quaint and the exotic. And it was this conservatism in Hearn that made him the most sympathetic, and perhaps the most penetrating, Western writer of the Japanese scene. For he shared with the old-fashioned Japanese, who still formed the greater part of the population, their respect for tradition, their love of the past, and their belief in things not of this world. He did not believe, as did the intolerant Western traders and the equally intolerant sectarian missionaries who had followed them, that ancestor worship was no more than mere heathen superstition. Gratitude to one's ancestors who had, through countless generations of toil, helped to make one's own life worth living, was not, he felt, an ignoble thing. Nor did he scoff at the peasants who still believed in ghosts. For he had once believed in ghosts and goblins too, and if he did not, in his maturity, quite believe in the existence of goblins, he did, like the Japanese peasants, feel deeply the close kinship between the living and the dead. In the credulous, kindly peasants, he found more wisdom and tolerance than in the modern Japanese from the city colleges, whose education had taught them little more than the crudest forms of Western skepticism. And he found the company of

Buddhist and Shinto priests, who were always hospitable to the shy, one-eyed stranger, more rewarding than that of his fellow university professors at Tokyo, many of whom seemed to resent his presence.

Hearn's enthusiasm for ghost-stories and fairy-tales was sometimes criticized by his upper-class Japanese acquaintances, who felt that his writings would create abroad the wrong impression of their country's culture. But Hearn saw nothing shameful about ghost-stories or fairy-tales. He thought them beautiful, and he was contemptuous of any Japanese who failed to see the great beauty of his own folk-lore.

These legends, which had haunted the Japanese for centuries, he heard from his Japanese wife, his friends, his servants, and chance acquaintances he made in his travels. Since he could not read Japanese, his renderings of them in English are not exactly translations. But he was a careful listener, and he often begged to be told a story over and over again, so that when he wrote it down, it might not lose that fine Japanese quality which characterizes the best of his tales. And often at night when the ghostly mood was upon him, he would tell the tales himself, and his friends would listen enthralled, wondering at this foreign friend of theirs, who knew their own ghosts and goblins better than they. Sometimes, the experience would haunt them for days on end, and they would remember how his eye had glistened in the half-darkness, and how pale his face had looked, and how, for a moment or two, they had almost thought that *he* was a ghost.

Hearn's ghost-stories, however, are not the most important part of his Japanese writings. In the fourteen years that he lived in Japan, a dozen or more of his books dealing with various aspects of her civilization were published. In these volumes, the reader will find, besides legends, impressionistic sketches of life in the towns and villages, studies of insects and native literature concerning them, and contemplative essays on Japanese history, religion, customs, and institutions. Though these volumes are unequal in quality, they form on the whole the most illuminating study of Japanese life ever made by a Westerner. It is true that he was not a scholar, in the manner of such men as Aston and Chamberlain, who knew Buddhist philosophy and Japan's great classics far better than he. But he knew far, far better than other Westerners what the Japanese thought and how they felt about their own past, their immemorial ways and institutions; and it is because he understood their thoughts and feelings so well that Hearn's books still remain the wisest, the most charming and gracious, the most fruitfully revealing of all those hundreds of books written in English about Japan.

His knowledge of the country, Hearn gained not so much from books, as from his close friends among the gentry, peasantry, and the priesthood; and if he did not know as well as some the intricacies of Buddhist doctrine, he knew as well as any the living faith of the people; or, if his knowledge of Japan's ancient history was not as thorough as it might have been, his knowledge of the ancient ways of life, as they were still being lived by his samurai and peasant friends, left little to be desired. Hearn knew that he lacked scholarly knowledge, and he felt—perhaps more keenly than he should—that this lack detracted from his value as an interpreter of Japanese culture. His shortcomings as a scholar, however, were more than compensated for by his great literary skill, which surpassed that of any other Englishman or American then living in Japan, and by his instinctive understanding of a reverent, tradition-loving people, which enabled him to see the beauty that they saw, and to feel the sadness that they felt, in a world that was passing.

". . . I should like," wrote Hearn, shortly before his death, "when my time comes, to be laid away in some Buddhist graveyard of the ancient kind,—so that my ghostly company should be ancient, caring nothing for the fashions and the changes and the disintegrations of Meiji. That old cemetery behind my garden would be a suitable place. Everything there is beautiful with a beauty of exceeding and startling queerness; each tree and stone has been shaped by some old, old ideal which no longer exists in any living brain; even the shadows are not of this time and sun, but of a world forgotten, . . ." But the great ancient trees in the temple grounds behind his house were cut down during the last days of his life, and when he died, he was not buried in the graveyard of his choice.

Hearn, and the many Japanese who thought and felt as he did, were virtually powerless against the civilized barbarisms that were sweeping the country, for they had not only Japanese innovators to contend with, but also the uncontrollable forces of the West.

Hearn knew only one way of helping to check the tide, and that was to remind the Japanese themselves of their great national heritage, and to interpret the character of this heritage to the people of the West. In his attempts at interpretation, Hearn wished to emphasize the uniqueness of Japanese civilization in this modern age, and to warn his readers that only by cherishing the beauty and variety of this world would they be able to check the *almost* resistless forces of ugliness and uniformity, forces here below which probably try God's patience beyond all others.

EDWIN McCLELLAN

CONTENTS

Introduction v

The Mirror of Matsuyama..................... 1

The Story of Mimi-Nashi-Hoichi.............. 3

Jiu-Roku-Zakura 16

Oshidori 18

The Reconciliation 21

Yuki-Onna 26

Of a Promise Kept......................... 32

The Dream of a Summer Day............... 37

A Conservative 56

Some Thoughts about Ancestor-Worship...... 82

The Nun of the Temple of Amida............110

In the Twilight of the Gods...............121

Otokichi's Daruma 130

Kusa-Hibari 138

Mosquitoes 143

Acknowledgments 147

THE MIRROR OF MATSUYAMA

Long ago, at a place called Matsuyama, in the province of Echigo, there lived a young samurai husband and wife whose names have been quite forgotten. They had a little daughter.

Once the husband went to Yedo,—probably as a retainer in the train of the Lord of Echigo. On his return he brought presents from the capital,—sweet cakes and a doll for the little girl, and for his wife a mirror of silvered bronze. To the young mother that mirror seemed a very wonderful thing; for it was the first mirror ever brought to Matsuyama. She did not understand the use of it, and innocently asked whose was the pretty smiling face she saw inside it. When the husband answered her, laughing, "Why, it is your own face! How foolish you are!" she was ashamed to ask any more questions, but hastened to put her present away, still thinking it to be a very mysterious thing. And she kept it hidden many years,—the original story does not say why. Perhaps for the simple reason that in all countries love makes even the most trifling gift too sacred to be shown.

But in the time of her last sickness she gave the mirror to her daughter, saying, "After I am dead you must look into this mirror every morning and evening, and you will see me. Do not grieve." Then she died.

And the girl thereafter looked into the mirror every morning and evening, and did not know that the face in the mirror was her own shadow,—but thought it to be that of her dead mother, whom she much resembled. So she would talk to the shadow, having the sensation, or, as the Japanese original more tenderly says, *"having the heart of meeting her mother"* day by day; and she prized the mirror above all things.

At last her father noticed this conduct, and thought it strange, and asked the reason of it, whereupon she told him all. "Then," says the old Japanese narrator, "he thinking it to be a very piteous thing, his eyes grew dark with tears."

THE STORY OF MIMI-NASHI-HOICHI

More than seven hundred years ago, at Dan-no-ura, in the Straits of Shimonoseki, was fought the last battle of the long contest between the Heike, or Taira clan, and the Genji, or Minamoto clan. There the Heike perished utterly, with their women and children, and their infant emperor likewise—now remembered as Antoku Tenno. And that sea and shore have been haunted for seven hundred years. . . . Elsewhere I told you about the strange crabs found there, called Heike crabs, which have human faces on their backs, and are said to be the spirits of Heike warriors.[1] But there are many strange things to be seen and heard along that coast. On dark nights thousands of ghostly fires hover about the beach, or flit above the waves,—pale lights which the fishermen call *Oni-bi*, or demon-fires; and, whenever the winds are up, a sound of great shouting comes from the sea, like a clamor of battle.

In former years the Heike were much more restless than they now are. They would rise about ships passing in the night, and try to sink them; and at all times they would watch for swimmers, to pull them down. It was in order to appease those dead that the Buddhist temple, Amidaji, was built at Akamagaseki.[2] A cemetery also was made close by, near the beach; and within it were set up monuments inscribed with the names of the drowned emperor and of his

---

1. See my *Kotto*, for a description of these curious crabs.
2. Or, Shimonoseki. The town is also known by the name of Bakkan.

great vassals; and Buddhist services were regularly performed there, on behalf of the spirits of them. After the temple had been built, and the tombs erected, the Heike gave less trouble than before; but they continued to do queer things at intervals,—proving that they had not found the perfect peace.

Some centuries ago there lived at Akamagaseki a blind man named Hoichi, who was famed for his skill in recitation and in playing upon the *biwa*.[3] From childhood he had been trained to recite and to play; and while yet a lad he had surpassed his teachers. As a professional *biwa-hoshi* he became famous chiefly by his recitations of the history of the Heike and the Genji; and it is said that when he sang the song of the battle of Dan-no-ura "even the goblins *(kijin)* could not refrain from tears."

At the outset of his career, Hoichi was very poor; but he found a good friend to help him. The priest of the Amidaji was fond of poetry and music; and he often invited Hoichi to the temple, to play and recite. Afterwards, being much impressed by the wonderful skill of the lad, the priest proposed that Hoichi should make the temple his home; and this offer was gratefully accepted. Hoichi was given a room in the temple-building; and in return for food and lodging, he was required only to gratify the priest

3. The *biwa*, a kind of four-stringed lute, is chiefly used in musical recitative. Formerly the professional minstrels who recited the *Heike-Monogatari*, and other tragical histories, were called *biwa-hoshi*, or "lute-priests." The origin of this appellation is not clear; but it is possible that it may have been suggested by the fact that "lute-priests," as well as blind shampooers, had their heads shaven, like Buddhist priests. The *biwa* is played with a kind of plectrum, called *bachi*, usually made of horn.

with a musical performance on certain evenings, when otherwise disengaged.

One summer night the priest was called away, to perform a Buddhist service at the house of a dead parishioner; and he went there with his acolyte, leaving Hoichi alone in the temple. It was a hot night; and the blind man sought to cool himself on the verandah before his sleeping-room. The verandah overlooked a small garden in the rear of the Amidaji. There Hoichi waited for the priest's return, and tried to relieve his solitude by practicing upon his biwa. Midnight passed; and the priest did not appear. But the atmosphere was still too warm for comfort within doors; and Hoichi remained outside. At last he heard steps approaching from the back gate. Somebody crossed the garden, advanced to the verandah, and halted directly in front of him—but it was not the priest. A deep voice called the blind man's name—abruptly and unceremoniously, in the manner of a samurai summoning an inferior:—

"Hoichi!"

Hoichi was much too startled, for the moment, to respond; and the voice called again, in a tone of harsh command,—

"Hoichi!"

"Hai!" answered the blind man, frightened by the menace in the voice,—"I am blind!—I cannot know who calls!"

"There is nothing to fear," the stranger exclaimed, speaking more gently. "I am stopping near this temple, and have been sent to you with a message. My present lord, a person of exceedingly high rank, is now staying in Akamagaseki, with many noble attendants. He wished to view the scene of the battle of Dan-no-ura; and today he visited that place. Having heard of your skill in reciting the story of the battle, he now desires to hear your performance: so you will take your biwa and come with me at once to the house where the august assembly is waiting."

In those times, the order of a samurai was not to be lightly disobeyed. Hoichi donned his sandals, took his biwa, and went away with the stranger, who guided him deftly, but obliged him to walk very fast. The hand that guided was iron; and the clank of the warrior's stride proved him fully armed,—probably some palace-guard on duty. Hoichi's first alarm was over: he began to imagine himself in good luck;—for, remembering the retainer's assurance about a "person of exceedingly high rank," he thought that the lord who wished to hear the recitation could not be less than a daimyo of the first class. Presently the samurai halted; and Hoichi became aware that they had arrived at a large gateway;—and he wondered, for he could not remember any large gate in that part of the town, except the main gate of the Amidaji. *"Kaimon!"*[1] the samurai called,—and there was a sound of unbarring; and the twain passed on. They traversed a space of garden, and halted again before some entrance; and the retainer cried in a loud voice, "Within there! I have brought Hoichi." Then came sounds of feet hurrying, and screens sliding, and rain-doors opening, and voices of women in converse. By the language of the women Hoichi knew them to be

1. A respectful term, signifying the opening of a gate. It was used by samurai when calling to the guards on duty at a lord's gate for admission.

domestics in some noble household; but he could not imagine to what place he had been conducted. Little time was allowed him for conjecture. After he had been helped to mount several stone steps, upon the last of which he was told to leave his sandals, a woman's hand guided him along interminable reaches of polished planking, and round pillared angles too many to remember, and over widths amazing of matted floor,—into the middle of some vast apartment. There he thought that many people were assembled: the sound of the rustling of silk was like the sound of leaves in a forest. He heard also a great humming of voices,—talking in undertones; and the speech was the speech of courts.

Hoichi was told to put himself at ease, and he found a kneeling-cushion ready for him. After having taken his place upon it, and tuned his instrument, the voice of a woman—whom he divined to be the *Rojo*, or matron in charge of the female service—addressed him, saying,—

"It is now required that the history of the Heike be recited, to the accompaniment of the biwa."

Now the entire recital would have required a time of many nights: therefore Hoichi ventured a question:—

"As the whole of the story is not soon told, what portion is it augustly desired that I now recite?"

The woman's voice made answer:—

"Recite the story of the battle at Dan-no-ura,—for the pity of it is the most deep."[1]

---

1. Or the phrase might be rendered, "for the pity of that part is the deepest." The Japanese word for pity in the original text is *aware*.

Then Hoichi lifted up his voice, and chanted the chant of the fight on the bitter sea,—wonderfully making his biwa to sound like the straining of oars and the rushing of ships, the whirr and the hissing of arrows, the shouting and trampling of men, the crashing of steel upon helmets, the plunging of slain in the flood. And to left and right of him, in the pauses of his playing, he could hear voices murmuring praise: "How marvelous an artist!"—"Never in our own province was playing heard like this!"—"Not in all the empire is there another singer like Hoichi!" Then fresh courage came to him, and he played and sang yet better than before; and a hush of wonder deepened about him. But when at last he came to tell of the fate of the fair and helpless,—the piteous perishing of the women and children,—and the death-leap of Nii-no-Ama, with the imperial infant in her arms,— then all the listeners uttered together one long, long shuddering cry of anguish; and thereafter they wept and wailed so loudly and so wildly that the blind man was frightened by the violence of the grief that he had made. For much time the sobbing and the wailing continued. But gradually the sounds of lamentation died away; and again, in the great stillness that followed, Hoichi heard the voice of the woman whom he supposed to be the Rojo.

She said:—

"Although we had been assured that you were a very skillful player upon the biwa, and without an equal in recitative, we did not know that anyone could be so skillful as you have proved yourself to-night. Our lord has been pleased to say that he intends to bestow upon you a fitting reward. But he desires that you shall perform before him once every night for the next six nights—after which time he will probably make his august return-journey. Tomorrow night, therefore, you are to come here at the same hour. The retainer who tonight conducted you will be sent for you. . . . There is another matter about which I have been ordered to inform you. It is required that you shall speak to no one of your visits here, during the time of our lord's august sojourn at Akamagaseki. As he is traveling incognito,[1] he commands that no mention of these things be made. . . . You are now free to go back to your temple."

After Hoichi had duly expressed his thanks, a woman's hand conducted him to the entrance of the house, where the same retainer, who had before guided him, was waiting to take him home. The retainer led him to the verandah at the rear of the temple, and there bade him farewell.

It was almost dawn when Hoichi returned; but his absence from the temple had not been observed,— as the priest, coming back at a very late hour, had supposed him asleep. During the day Hoichi was able to take some rest; and he said nothing about his strange adventure. In the middle of the following night the samurai came again for him, and led him to the august assembly, where he gave another recitation with the same success that had attended his previous performance. But during this second visit his absence from the temple was accidentally dis-

---

1. "Traveling incognito" is at least the meaning of the original phrase,—"making a disguised august-journey" (shinobi no go-ryoko).

covered; and after his return in the morning he was summoned to the presence of the priest, who said to him, in a tone of kindly reproach:—

"We have been very anxious about you, friend Hoichi. To go out, blind and alone, at so late an hour, is dangerous. Why did you go without telling us? I could have ordered a servant to accompany you. And where have you been?"

Hoichi answered, evasively,—

"Pardon me, kind friend! I had to attend to some private business; and I could not arrange the matter at any other hour."

The priest was surprised, rather than pained, by Hoichi's reticence: he felt it to be unnatural, and suspected something wrong. He feared that the blind lad had been bewitched or deluded by some evil spirits. He did not ask any more questions; but he privately instructed the men-servants of the temple to keep watch upon Hoichi's movements, and to follow him in case that he should again leave the temple after dark.

On the very next night, Hoichi was seen to leave the temple; and the servants immediately lighted their lanterns, and followed after him. But it was a rainy night, and very dark; and before the temple-folks could get to the roadway, Hoichi had disappeared. Evidently he had walked very fast,—a strange thing, considering his blindness; for the road was in a bad condition. The men hurried through the streets, making inquiries at every house which Hoichi was accustomed to visit; but nobody could give them any news of him. At last, as they were returning to

the temple by way of the shore, they were startled by
the sound of a biwa, furiously played in the cemetery
of the Amidaji. Except for some ghostly fires—
such as usually flitted there on dark nights—all was
blackness in that direction. But the men at once
hastened to the cemetery; and there, by the help of
their lanterns, they discovered Hoichi,—sitting alone
in the rain before the memorial tomb of Antoku
Tenno, making his biwa resound, and loudly chanting
the chant of the battle of Dan-no-ura. And behind
him, and about him, and everywhere above the
tombs, the fires of the dead were burning, like candles. Never before had so great a host of *Oni-bi* appeared in the sight of mortal man. . . .

"Hoichi San!—Hoichi San!" the servants cried,—
"you are bewitched! . . . Hoichi San!"

But the blind man did not seem to hear. Strenu-
ously he made his biwa to rattle and ring and
clang;—more and more wildly he chanted the chant
of the battle of Dan-no-ura. They caught hold of
him;—they shouted into his ear,—

"Hoichi San!—Hoichi San!—come home with us
at once!"

Reprovingly he spoke to them:—

"To interrupt me in such a manner, before this
august assembly, will not be tolerated."

Whereat, in spite of the weirdness of the thing, the
servants could not help laughing. Sure that he had
been bewitched, they now seized him, and pulled him
up on his feet, and by main force hurried him back
to the temple,—where he was immediately relieved
of his wet clothes, by order of the priest, and reclad,
and made to eat and drink. Then the priest insisted

upon a full explanation of his friend's astonishing behavior.

Hoichi long hesitated to speak. But at last, finding that his conduct had really alarmed and angered the good priest, he decided to abandon his reserve; and he related everything that had happened from the time of the first visit of the samurai.

The priest said:—

"Hoichi, my poor friend, you are now in great danger! How unfortunate that you did not tell me all this before! Your wonderful skill in music has indeed brought you into strange trouble. By this time you must be aware that you have not been visiting any house whatever, but have been passing your nights in the cemetery, among the tombs of the Heike;—and it was before the memorial-tomb of Antoku Tenno that our people tonight found you, sitting in the rain. All that you have been imagining was illusion—except the calling of the dead. By once obeying them, you have put yourself in their power. If you obey them again, after what has already occurred, they will tear you in pieces. But they would have destroyed you, sooner or later, in any event. . . . Now I shall not be able to remain with you tonight: I am called away to perform another service. But, before I go, it will be necessary to protect your body by writing holy texts upon it."

Before sundown the priest and his acolyte stripped Hoichi: then, with their writing-brushes, they traced upon his breast and back, head and face and neck, limbs and hands and feet,—even upon the soles of his feet, and upon all parts of his body,—the text of the holy sutra called *Hannya-Shin-Kyo*. When this had been done, the priest instructed Hoichi, saying:—

"Tonight, as soon as I go away, you must seat yourself on the verandah, and wait. You will be called. But, whatever may happen, do not answer, and do not move. Say nothing, and sit still—as if meditating. If you stir, or make any noise, you will be torn asunder. Do not get frightened; and do not think of calling for help—because no help could save you. If you do exactly as I tell you, the danger will pass, and you will have nothing more to fear."

After dark the priest and the acolyte went away; and Hoichi seated himself on the verandah, according to the instructions given him. He laid his biwa on the planking beside him, and, assuming the attitude of meditation, remained quite still,—taking care not to cough, or to breathe audibly. For hours he stayed thus.

Then, from the roadway, he heard the steps coming. They passed the gate, crossed the garden, approached the verandah, stopped—directly in front of him.

"Hoichi!" the deep voice called. But the blind man held his breath, and sat motionless.

"Hoichi!" grimly called the voice a second time. Then a third time—savagely:—

"Hoichi!"

Hoichi remained as still as a stone,—and the voice grumbled:—

"No answer!—that won't do! . . . Must see where the fellow is.". . .

There was a noise of heavy feet mounting upon the verandah. The feet approached deliberately,—and halted beside him. Then, for long minutes,—during which Hoichi felt his whole body shake to the beating of his heart,—there was dead silence.

At last the gruff voice muttered close to him:—

"Here is the biwa; but of the biwa-player I see— only two ears! . . . So that explains why he did not answer: he had no mouth to answer with—there is nothing left of him but his ears. . . . Now to my lord those ears I will take—in proof that the august commands have been obeyed, so far as was possible". . .

At that instant Hoichi felt his ears gripped by fingers of iron, and torn off! Great as the pain was, he gave no cry. The heavy footfalls receded along the verandah,—descended into the garden,—passed out to the roadway,—ceased. From either side of his head, the blind man felt a thick warm trickling; but he dared not lift his hands. . . .

Before sunrise the priest came back. He hastened at once to the verandah in the rear, stepped and slipped upon something clammy, and uttered a cry of horror;—for he saw, by the light of his lantern, that the clamminess was blood. But he perceived Hoichi sitting there, in the attitude of meditation— with the blood still oozing from his wounds.

"My poor Hoichi!" cried the startled priest,— "what is this? . . . You have been hurt?" . . .

At the sound of his friend's voice, the blind man felt safe. He burst out sobbing, and tearfully told his adventure of the night.

"Poor, poor Hoichi!" the priest exclaimed.—"all my fault!—my very grievous fault! . . . Everywhere upon your body the holy texts had been written—except upon your ears! I trusted my acolyte to do that part of the work; and it was very, very wrong of me not to have made sure that he had done it! . . . Well, the matter cannot now be helped;— we can only try to heal your hurts as soon as possible. . . . Cheer up, friend!—the danger is now well over. You will never again be troubled by those visitors."

With the aid of a good doctor, Hoichi soon recovered from his injuries. The story of his strange adventure spread far and wide, and soon made him famous. Many noble persons went to Akamagaseki to hear him recite; and large presents of money were given to him,—so that he became a wealthy man. . . . But from the time of his adventure, he was known only by the appellation of *Mimi-nashi-Hoichi*: "Hoichi-the-Earless."

JIU-ROKU-ZAKURA

In Wakegori, a district of the province of Iyo, there is a very ancient and famous cherry-tree, called *Jiu-roku-zakura*, or "the Cherry-tree of the Sixteenth Day," because it blooms every year upon the sixteenth day of the first month (by the old lunar calendar),—and only upon that day. Thus the time of its flowering is the Period of Great Cold,—though the natural habit of a cherry-tree is to wait for the spring season before venturing to blossom. But the *Jiu-roku-zakura* blossoms with a life that is not—or, at least, was not originally—its own. There is the ghost of a man in that tree.

He was a samurai of Iyo; and the tree grew in his garden; and it used to flower at the usual time,— that is to say, about the end of March or the beginning of April. He had played under that tree when he was a child; and his parents and grandparents and ancestors had hung to its blossoming branches, season after season for more than a hundred years, bright strips of colored paper inscribed with poems of praise. He himself became very old,—outliving all his children; and there was nothing in the world left for him to love except that tree. And lo! in the summer of a certain year, the tree withered and died!

Exceedingly the old man sorrowed for his tree. Then kind neighbors found for him a young and beautiful cherry-tree, and planted it in his garden,— hoping thus to comfort him. And he thanked them, and pretended to be glad. But really his heart was full of pain; for he had loved the old tree so well that nothing could have consoled him for the loss of it.

At last there came to him a happy thought: He remembered a way by which the perishing tree might be saved. (It was the sixteenth day of the first month.) Alone he went into his garden, and bowed before the withered tree, and spoke to it, saying: "Now deign, I beseech you, once more to bloom,— because I am going to die in your stead." For it is believed that one can really give away one's life to another person, or to a creature, or even to a tree, by the favor of the gods;—and thus to transfer one's life is expressed by the term *migawari ni tatsu,* "to act as a substitute.") Then under that tree he spread a white cloth, and divers coverings, and sat down upon the coverings, and performed *hara-kiri* after the fashion of a samurai. And the ghost of him went into the tree, and made it blossom in that same hour.

And every year it still blooms on the sixteenth day of the first month, in the season of snow.

OSHIDORI

There was a falconer and hunter, named Sonjo,
who lived in the district called Tamura-no-Go, of the
province of Mutsu. One day he went out hunting,
and could not find any game. But on his way home,
at a place called Akanuma, he perceived a pair of
oshidori[1] (mandarin-ducks), swimming together in
a river that he was about to cross. To kill *oshidori*
is not good; but Sonjo happened to be very hungry,
and he shot at the pair. His arrow pierced the male:
the female escaped into the rushes of the further
shore, and disappeared. Sonjo took the dead bird
home, and cooked it.

That night he dreamed a dreary dream. It seemed
to him that a beautiful woman came into his room,
and stood by his pillow, and began to weep. So bitterly did she weep that Sonjo felt as if his heart were
being torn out while he listened. And the woman
cried to him: "Why,—oh! why did you kill him?—
of what wrong was he guilty? . . . At Akanuma we
were so happy together,—and you killed him! . . .
What harm did he ever do you? Do you even know
what you have done?—oh! do you know what a
cruel, what a wicked thing you have done? . . . Me
too you have killed,—for I will not live without my
husband! . . . Only to tell you this I came." . . .
Then again she wept aloud,—so bitterly that the

---

1. From ancient time, in the Far East, these birds have been regarded as emblems of conjugal affection.

voice of her crying pierced into the marrow of the listener's bones;—and she sobbed out the words of this poem:—

Hi kurureba
Sasoeshi mono wo —
Akanuma no
Makomo no kure no
Hitori-ne zo uki!

("At the coming of twilight I invited him to return with me—! Now to sleep alone in the shadow of the rushes of Akanuma—ah! what misery unspeakable!")

And after having uttered these verses she exclaimed:—"Ah, you do not know—you cannot know what you have done! But to-morrow, when you go to Akanuma, you will see. . . ." So saying, and weeping very piteously, she went away.

When Sonjo awoke in the morning, this dream remained so vivid in his mind that he was greatly troubled. He remembered the words:—"But to-morrow, when you go to Akanuma, you will see,— you will see." And he resolved to go there at once, that he might learn whether his dream was anything more than a dream.

So he went to Akanuma; and there, when he came to the river-bank, he saw the female *oshidori* swimming alone. In the same moment the bird perceived Sonjo; but, instead of trying to escape, she swam straight towards him, looking at him the while in a strange fixed way. Then, with her beak, she suddenly tore open her own body, and died before the hunter's eyes. . . .

Sonjo shaved his head, and became a priest.

THE RECONCILIATION

There was a young Samurai of Kyoto who had been reduced to poverty by the ruin of his lord, and found himself obliged to leave his home, and to take service with the Governor of a distant province. Before quitting the capital, this Samurai divorced his wife,—a good and beautiful woman,—under the belief that he could obtain better promotion by another alliance. He then married the daughter of a family of some distinction, and took her with him to the district whither he had been called.

But it was in the time of the thoughtlessness of youth, and the sharp experience of want, that the Samurai could not understand the worth of the affection so lightly cast away. His second marriage did not prove a happy one; the character of his new wife was hard and selfish; and he soon found every cause to think with regret of Kyoto days. Then he discovered that he still loved his first wife—loved her more than he could ever love the second; and he began to feel how unjust and how thankless he had been. Gradually his repentance deepened into a remorse that left him no peace of mind. Memories of the woman he had wronged—her gentle speech, her smiles, her dainty, pretty ways, her faultless patience —continually haunted him. Sometimes in dreams he saw her at her loom, weaving as when she toiled night and day to help him during the years of their distress: more often he saw her kneeling alone in the desolate little room where he had left her, veiling her tears

with her poor worn sleeve. Even in the hours of
official duty, his thoughts would wander back to her:
then he would ask himself how she was living, what
she was doing. Something in his heart assured him
that she could not accept another husband, and that
she never would refuse to pardon him. And he secret-
ly resolved to seek her out as soon as he could return
to Kyoto,—then to beg her forgiveness, to take her
back, to do everything that a man could do to make
atonement. But the years went by.

At last the Governor's official term expired, and
the Samurai was free. "Now I will go back to my
dear one," he vowed to himself. "Ah, what a cruelty,
—what a folly to have divorced her!" He sent his
second wife to her own people (she had given him
no children); and hurrying to Kyoto, he went at once
to seek his former companion,—not allowing himself
even the time to change his traveling-garb.

When he reached the street where she used to live,
it was late in the night,—the night of the tenth day
of the ninth month;—and the city was silent as a
cemetery. But a bright moon made everything visible; and he found the house without difficulty. It had
a deserted look: tall weeds were growing on the roof.
He knocked at the sliding-doors, and no-one answered. Then, finding that the doors had not been
fastened from within, he pushed them open, and
entered. The front room was matless and empty: a
chilly wind was blowing through crevices in the
planking; and the moon shone through a ragged
break in the wall of the alcove. Other rooms pre-

sented a like forlorn condition. The house, to all seeming, was unoccupied. Nevertheless, the Samurai determined to visit one other apartment at the further end of the dwelling,—a very small room that had been his wife's favorite resting-place. Approaching the sliding-screen that closed it, he was startled to perceive a glow within. He pushed the screen aside, and uttered a cry of joy; for he saw her there,—sewing by the light of a paper lamp. Her eyes at the same instant met his own; and with a happy smile she greeted him,—asking only:—"When did you come back to Kyoto? How did you find your way here to me, through all those black rooms?" The years had not changed her. She still seemed as fair and young as in his fondest memory of her;—but sweeter than any memory there came to him the music of her voice, with its trembling of pleased wonder.

Then joyfully he took his place beside her, and told her all:—how deeply he repented his selfishness,—how wretched he had been without her,—how constantly he had regretted her,—how long he had hoped and planned to make amends;—caressing her the while, and asking her forgiveness over and over again. She answered him, with loving gentleness, according to his heart's desire,—entreating him to cease all self-reproach. It was wrong, she said, that he should have allowed himself to suffer on her account: she had always felt that she was not worthy to be his wife. She knew that he had separated from her, notwithstanding, only because of poverty; and while he lived with her, he had always been kind; and she had never ceased to pray for his happiness.

But even if there had been a reason for speaking of amends, this honorable visit would be ample amends;—what greater happiness than thus to see him again, though it were only for a moment? "Only for a moment!" he answered, with a glad laugh,— "say, rather, for the time of seven existences! My loved one, unless you forbid, I am coming back to live with you always—always—always! Nothing shall ever separate us again. Now I have means and friends: we need not fear poverty. To-morrow my goods will be brought here; and my servants will come to wait upon you; and we shall make this house beautiful. . . . To-night," he added, apologetically, "I came thus late—without even changing my dress—only because of the longing I had to see you, and to tell you this." She seemed greatly pleased by these words; and in her turn she told him about all that had happened in Kyoto since the time of his departure,—excepting her own sorrows, of which she sweetly refused to speak. They chatted far into the night: then she conducted him to a warmer room, facing south,—a room that had been their bridal chamber in former time. "Have you no one in the house to help you?" he asked, as she began to prepare the couch for him. "No," she answered, laughing cheerfully: "I could not afford a servant;—so I have been living all alone." "You will have plenty of servants to-morrow," he said,—"good servants,— and everything else that you need." They lay down to rest,—not to sleep: they had too much to tell each other;—and they talked of the past and the present and the future, until the dawn was grey. Then, in-voluntarily, the Samurai closed his eyes, and slept.

When he awoke, the daylight was streaming through the chinks of the sliding-shutters; and he found himself, to his utter amazement, lying upon the naked boards of a mouldering floor. . . . Had he only dreamed a dream? No: She was there;—she slept. . . . He bent above her,—and looked,—and shrieked;—for the sleeper had no face! . . . Before him, wrapped in its grave-sheet only, lay the corpse of a woman,—a corpse so wasted that little remained save the bones, and the long tangled black hair.

.   .   .   .

Slowly,—as he stood shuddering and sickening in the sun,—the icy horror yielded to a despair so intolerable, a pain so atrocious, that he clutched at the mocking doubt. Feigning ignorance of the neighborhood, he ventured to ask the way to the house in which his wife had lived.

"There is no-one in that house," said the person questioned. "It used to belong to the wife of a Samurai who left the city several years ago. He divorced her in order to marry another woman before he went away; and she fretted a great deal, and so became sick. She had no relatives in Kyoto, and nobody to care for her; and she died in the autumn of the same year,—on the tenth day of the ninth month. . . ."

YUKI-ONNA

In a village of Musashi Province, there lived two woodcutters: Mosaku and Minokichi. At the time of which I am speaking, Mosaku was an old man; and Minokichi, his apprentice, was a lad of eighteen years. Every day they went together to a forest situated about five miles from their village. On the way to that forest there is a wide river to cross; and there is a ferryboat. Several times a bridge was built where the ferry is; but the bridge was each time carried away by a flood. No common bridge can resist the current there when the river rises.

Mosaku and Minokichi were on their way home, one very cold evening, when a great snowstorm overtook them. They reached the ferry; and they found that the boatman had gone away, leaving his boat on the other side of the river. It was no day for swimming; and the woodcutters took shelter in the ferryman's hut,—thinking themselves lucky to find any shelter at all. There was no brazier in the hut, nor any place in which to make a fire: it was only a two-mat[1] hut, with a single door, but no window. Mosaku and Minokichi fastened the door, and lay down to rest, with their straw rain-coats over them. At first they did not feel very cold; and they thought that the storm would soon be over.

The old man almost immediately fell asleep; but the boy, Minokichi, lay awake a long time, listening

1. That is to say, with a floor-surface of about six feet square.

to the awful wind, and the continual slashing of the snow against the door. The river was roaring; and the hut swayed and creaked like a junk at sea. It was a terrible storm; and the air was every moment becoming colder; and Minokichi shivered under his rain-coat. But at last, in spite of the cold, he too fell asleep.

He was awakened by a showering of snow in his face. The door of the hut had been forced open; and, by the snow-light *(yuki-akari)*, he saw a woman in the room,—a woman all in white. She was bending above Mosaku, and blowing her breath upon him;— and her breath was like a bright white smoke. Almost in the same moment she turned to Minokichi, and stooped over him. He tried to cry out, but found that he could not utter any sound. The white woman bent down over him, lower and lower, until her face almost touched him; and he saw that she was very beautiful,—though her eyes made him afraid. For a little time she continued to look at him;—then she smiled, and she whispered:—"I intended to treat you like the other man. But I cannot help feeling some pity for you,—because you are so young. . . . You are a pretty boy, Minokichi; and I will not hurt you now. But, if you ever tell anybody—even your own mother—about what you have seen this night, I shall know it; and then I will kill you. . . . Remember what I say!"

With these words, she turned from him, and passed through the doorway. Then he found himself able to move; and he sprang up, and looked out. But the woman was nowhere to be seen; and the snow was driving furiously into the hut. Minokichi

closed the door, and secured it by fixing several
billets of wood against it. He wondered if the wind
had blown it open;—he thought that he might have
been only dreaming, and might have mistaken the
gleam of the snow-light in the doorway for the figure
of a white woman: but he could not be sure. He
called to Mosaku, and was frightened because the
old man did not answer. He put out his hand in the
dark, and touched Mosaku's face, and found that it
was ice! Mosaku was stark and dead. . . .

By dawn the storm was over; and when the ferryman returned to his station, a little after sunrise, he
found Minokichi lying senseless beside the frozen
body of Mosaku. Minokichi was promptly cared
for, and soon came to himself; but he remained a
long time ill from the effects of the cold of that terrible night. He had been greatly frightened also by
the old man's death; but he said nothing about the
vision of the woman in white. As soon as he got well
again, he returned to his calling,—going alone every
morning to the forest, and coming back at nightfall
with his bundles of wood, which his mother helped
him to sell.

One evening, in the winter of the following year, as
he was on his way home, he overtook a girl who
happened to be traveling by the same road. She was
a tall, slim girl, very good-looking; and she answered
Minokichi's greeting in a voice as pleasant to the
ear as the voice of a song-bird. Then he walked
beside her; and they began to talk. The girl said that

her name was O-Yuki;[1] that she had lately lost both
of her parents; and that she was going to Yedo,
where she happened to have some poor relations,
who might help her to find a situation as servant.
Minokichi soon felt charmed by this strange girl; and
the more he looked at her, the handsomer she appeared to be. He asked her whether she was yet be-
trothed; and she answered, laughingly, that she was
free. Then, in her turn, she asked Minokichi whether
he was married, or pledged to marry; and he told her
that, although he had only a widowed mother to
support, the question of an "honorable daughter-in-
law" had not yet been considered, as he was very
young. . . . After these confidences, they walked
on for a long while without speaking; but, as the
proverb declares, *Ki ga areha, me mo kuchi ni mono
wo iu*: "When the wish is there, the eyes can say as
much as the mouth." By the time they reached the
village, they had become very much pleased with
each other; and then Minokichi asked O-Yuki to rest
awhile at his house. After some shy hesitation, she
went there with him; and his mother made her welcome, and prepared a warm meal for her. O-Yuki
behaved so nicely that Minokichi's mother took a
sudden fancy to her, and persuaded her to delay her
journey to Yedo. And the natural end to the matter
was that O-Yuki never went to Yedo at all. She
remained in the house, as an "honorable daughter-
in-law."

---

1. This name, signifying "Snow" is not uncommon. On the subject
of Japanese female names, see my paper in the volume entitled
Shadowings.

O-Yuki proved a very good daughter-in-law. When Minokichi's mother came to die,—some five years later,—her last words were words of affection and praise for the wife of her son. And O-Yuki bore Minokichi ten children, boys and girls,—handsome children all of them, and very fair of skin.

The country-folk thought O-Yuki a wonderful person, by nature different from themselves. Most of the peasant-women age early; but O-Yuki, even after having become the mother of ten children, looked as young and fresh as on the day when she had first come to the village.

One night, after the children had gone to sleep, O-Yuki was sewing by the light of a paper lamp; and Minokichi, watching her, said:—

"To see you sewing there, with the light on your face, makes me think of a strange thing that happened when I was a lad of eighteen. I then saw somebody as beautiful and white as you are now—indeed, she was very like you." . . .

Without lifting her eyes from her work, O-Yuki responded:—

"Tell me about her. . . . Where did you see her?"

Then Minokichi told her about the terrible night in the ferryman's hut,—and about the White Woman that had stooped above him, smiling and whispering,—and about the silent death of old Mosaku. And he said:—

"Asleep or awake, that was the only time that I saw a being as beautiful as you. Of course, she was not a human being; and I was afraid of her,—very much afraid,—but she was so white! . . . Indeed, I have never been sure whether it was a dream that I saw, or the Woman of the Snow." . . .

O-Yuki flung down her sewing, and arose, and bowed above Minokichi where he sat, and shrieked into his face:—

"It was I—I—I! Yuki it was! And I told you then that I would kill you if you ever said one word about it! . . . But for those children asleep there, I would kill you this moment! And now you had better take very, very good care of them; for if ever they have reason to complain of you, I will treat you as you deserve!" . . .

Even as she screamed, her voice became thin, like a crying of wind;—then she melted into a bright white mist that spired to the roof-beams, and shuddered away through the smoke-hole. . . . Never again was she seen.

OF A PROMISE KEPT

"I shall return in the early autumn," said Akana Soyemon several hundred years ago,—when bidding good-bye to his brother by adoption, young Hasebe Samon. The time was spring; and the place was the village of Kato in the province of Harima. Akana was an Izumo samurai; and he wanted to visit his birthplace.

Hasebe said:—

"Your Izumo,—the Country of the Eight-Cloud Rising, is very distant. Perhaps it will therefore be difficult for you to promise to return here upon a particular day. But, if we were to know the exact day, we should feel happier. We could then prepare a feast of welcome; and we could watch at the gateway for your coming."

"Why, as for that," responded Akana, "I have been so much accustomed to travel that I can usually tell beforehand how long it will take me to reach a place; and I can safely promise you to be here upon a particular day. Suppose we say the day of the festival Choyo?"

"That is the ninth day of the ninth month," said Hasebe; — "then the chrysanthemums will be in bloom, and we can go together to look at them. How pleasant! . . . So you promise to come back on the ninth day of the ninth month?"

"On the ninth day of the ninth month," repeated Akana, smiling farewell. Then he strode away from the village of Kato in the province of Harima;—

and Hasebe Samon and the mother of Hasebe looked after him with tears in their eyes.

"Neither the Sun nor the Moon," says an old Japanese proverb, "ever halt upon their journey." Swiftly the months went by; and the autumn came,—the season of chrysanthemums. And early upon the morning of the ninth day of the ninth month Hasebe prepared to welcome his adopted brother. He made ready a feast of good things, bought wine, decorated the guest-room, and filled the vases of the alcove with chrysanthemums of two colors. Then his mother, watching him, said:—"The province of Izumo, my son, is more than one hundred *ri*[1] from this place; and the journey thence over the mountains is difficult and weary; and you cannot be sure that Akana will be able to come to-day. Would it not be better, before you take all this trouble, to wait for his coming?" "Nay, mother!" Hasebe made answer—"Akana promised to be here to-day: he could not break a promise! And if he were to see us beginning to make preparation after his arrival, he would know that we had doubted his word; and we should be put to shame."

The day was beautiful, the sky without a cloud, and the air so pure that the world seemed to be a thousand miles wider than usual. In the morning many travelers passed through the village—some of them samurai; and Hasebe, watching each as he came, more than once imagined that he saw Akana approaching. But the temple-bells sounded the hour

---

1. A *ri* is about equal to two and a half English miles.

of midday; and Akana did not appear. Through the afternoon also Hasebe watched and waited in vain. The sun set; and still there was no sign of Akana. Nevertheless Hasebe remained at the gate, gazing down the road. Later his mother went to him, and said: — "The mind of a man, my son, — as our proverb declares—may change as quickly as the sky of autumn. But your chrysanthemum-flowers will still be fresh to-morrow. Better now to sleep; and in the morning you can watch again for Akana, if you wish." "Rest well, mother," returned Hasebe;— "but I still believe that he will come." Then the mother went to her own room; and Hasebe lingered at the gate.

The night was pure as the day had been: all the sky throbbed with stars; and the white River of Heaven shimmered with unusual splendor. The village slept;—the silence was broken only by the noise of a little brook, and by the far-away barking of peasants' dogs. Hasebe still waited,—waited until he saw the thin moon sink behind the neighboring hills. Then at last he began to doubt and to fear. Just as he was about to re-enter the house, he perceived in the distance a tall man approaching,—very lightly and quickly; and in the next moment he recognized Akana.

"Oh!" cried Hasebe, springing to meet him—"I have been waiting for you from the morning until now! . . . So you really did keep your promise after all. . . . But you must be tired, poor brother! —come in;—everything is ready for you." He guided Akana to the place of honor in the guest-room, and hastened to trim the lights, which were burning low. "Mother," continued Hasebe, "felt a little tired this evening, and she has already gone to bed; but I shall awaken her presently." Akana shook his head, and made a little gesture of disapproval. "As you will, brother," said Hasebe; and he set warm food and wine before the traveler. Akana did not touch the food or the wine, but remained motionless and silent for a short time. Then, speaking in a whisper,—as if fearful of awakening the mother, he said:—

"Now I must tell you how it happened that I came thus late. When I returned to Izumo I found that the people had almost forgotten the kindness of our former ruler, the good Lord Enya, and were seeking the favor of the usurper Tsunehisa, who has possessed himself of the Tonda Castle. But I had to visit my cousin, Akana Tanji, though he had accepted service under Tsunehisa, and was living, as a retainer, within the castle grounds. He persuaded me to present myself before Tsunehisa: I yielded chiefly in order to observe the character of the new ruler, whose face I had never seen. He is a skilled soldier, and of great courage; but he is cunning and cruel. I found it necessary to let him know that I could never enter his service. After I left his presence he ordered my cousin to detain me—to keep me confined within the house. I protested that I had promised to return to Harima on the ninth day of the ninth month; but I was refused permission to go. I then hoped to escape from the castle at night; but I was constantly watched; and until to-day I could find no way to fulfill my promise. . . ."

"Until to-day!" exclaimed Hasebe in bewilderment;—"the castle is more than a hundred *ri* from here!"

"Yes," returned Akana; "and no living man can travel on foot a hundred *ri* in one day. But I felt that, if I did not keep my promise, you could not think well of me; and I remembered the ancient proverb, *Tama yoku ichi nichi ni sen ri wo yuku* ("The soul of a man can journey a thousand *ri* in a day"). Fortunately I had been allowed to keep my sword;—thus only was I able to come to you. . . . Be good to our mother."

With these words he stood up, and the same instant disappeared.

Then Hasebe knew that Akana had killed himself in order to fulfill the promise.

At earliest dawn Hasebe Samon set out for the Castle Tonda, in the province of Izumo. Reaching Matsue, he learned that, on the night of the ninth day of the ninth month, Akana Soyemon had performed *harakiri* in the house of Akana Tanji, in the grounds of the castle. Then Hasebe went to the house of Akana Tanji, and reproached Akana Tanji for the treachery done, and slew him in the midst of his family, and escaped without hurt. And when the Lord Tsunehisa had heard the story, he gave commands that Hasebe should not be pursued. For, although an unscrupulous and cruel man himself, the Lord Tsunehisa could respect the love of truth in others, and could admire the friendship and the courage of Hasebe Samon.

THE DREAM OF A SUMMER DAY

The hotel seemed to me a paradise, and the maids thereof celestial beings. This was because I had just fled away from one of the Open Ports, where I had ventured to seek comfort in a European hotel, supplied with all "modern improvements." To find myself at ease once more in a yukata,[1] seated upon cool, soft matting, waited upon by sweet-voiced girls, and surrounded by things of beauty, was therefore like a redemption from all the sorrows of the nineteenth century. Bamboo-shoots and lotus-bulbs were given me for breakfast, and a fan from heaven for a keepsake. The design upon that fan represented only the white rushing burst of one great wave on a beach, and sea-birds shooting in exultation through the blue overhead. But to behold it was worth all the trouble of the journey. It was a glory of light, a thunder of motion, a triumph of sea-wind,—all in one. It made me want to shout when I looked at it.

Between the cedarn balcony pillars I could see the course of the pretty gray town following the shore-sweep,—and yellow lazy junks asleep at anchor,—and the opening of the bay between enormous green cliffs,—and beyond it the blaze of summer to the horizon. In that horizon there were mountain shapes faint as old memories. And all things but the gray town, and the yellow junks, and the green cliffs, were blue.

Then a voice softly toned as a wind-bell began to tinkle words of courtesy into my reverie, and broke

---

1. A light kimono.

it; and I perceived that the mistress of the palace had come to thank me for the chadai,[2] and I prostrated myself before her. She was very young, and more than pleasant to look upon,—like the moth-maidens, like the butterfly-women, of Kunisada. And I thought at once of death;—for the beautiful is sometimes a sorrow of anticipation.

She asked whither I honorably intended to go, that she might order a kuruma for me. And I made answer:—

"To Kumamoto. But the name of your house I much wish to know, that I may always remember it."

"My guest-rooms," she said, "are augustly insignificant, and my maidens honorably rude. But the house is called the House of Urashima. And now I go to order a kuruma."

The music of her voice passed; and I felt enchantment falling all about me,—like the thrilling of a ghostly web. For the name was the name of the story of a song that bewitches men.

II

Once you hear the story, you will never be able to forget it. Every summer when I find myself on the coast,—especially on very soft, still days,—it haunts me most persistently. There are many native versions of it which have been the inspiration for countless works of art. But the most impressive and the most ancient is found in the "Manyefushifu," a collection of poems dating from the fifth to the ninth century.

---

[2] A little gift of money, always made to a hotel by the guest shortly after his arrival.

From this ancient version the great scholar Aston translated it into prose, and the great scholar Chamberlain into both prose and verse. But for English readers I think the most charming form of it is Chamberlain's version written for children, in the "Japanese Fairy-Tale Series,"—because of the delicious colored pictures by native artists. With that little book before me, I shall try to tell the legend over again in my own words.

Fourteen hundred and sixteen years ago, the fisher-boy Urashima Taro left the shore of Suminoye in his boat.

Summer days were then as now,—all drowsy and tender blue, with only some light, pure white clouds hanging over the mirror of the sea. Then, too, were the hills the same,—far blue soft shapes melting into the blue sky. And the winds were lazy.

And presently the boy, also lazy, let his boat drift as he fished. It was a queer boat, unpainted and rudderless, of a shape you probably never saw. But still, after fourteen hundred years, there are such boats to be seen in front of the ancient fishing-hamlets of the coast of the Sea of Japan.

After long waiting, Urashima caught something, and drew it up to him. But he found it was only a tortoise.

Now a tortoise is sacred to the Dragon God of the Sea, and the period of its natural life is a thousand—some say ten thousand—years. So that to kill it is very wrong. The boy gently unfastened the creature from his line, and set it free, with a prayer to the gods.

But he caught nothing more. And the day was very warm; and sea and air and all things were very, very silent. And a great drowsiness grew upon him,—and he slept in his drifting boat.

Then out of the dreaming of the sea rose up a beautiful girl,—just as you can see her in the picture to Professor Chamberlain's "Urashima,"—robed in crimson and blue, with long black hair flowing down her back even to her feet, after the fashion of a prince's daughter fourteen hundred years ago.

Gliding over the waters she came, softly as air; and she stood above the sleeping boy in the boat, and woke him with a light touch, and said:—

"Do not be surprised. My father, the Dragon King of the Sea, sent me to you, because of your kind heart. For today you set free a tortoise. And now we will go to my father's palace in the island where summer never dies; and I will be your flower-wife if you wish; and we shall live there happily forever."

And Urashima wondered more and more as he looked upon her; for she was more beautiful than any human being, and he could not but love her. Then she took one oar, and he took another, and they rowed away together,—just as you may still see, off the far western coast, wife and husband rowing together, when the fishing-boats flit into the evening gold.

They rowed away softly and swiftly over the silent blue water down into the south,—till they came to the island where summer never dies,—and to the palace of the Dragon King of the Sea.

(Here the text of the little book suddenly shrinks away as you read, and faint blue ripplings flood the page; and beyond them in a fairy horizon you can see the long low soft shore of the island, and peaked roofs rising through evergreen foliage—the roofs of the Sea God's palace—like the palace of the Mikado Yuriaku, fourteen hundred and sixteen years ago.)

There strange servitors came to receive them in robes of ceremony—creatures of the Sea, who paid greeting to Urashima as the son-in-law of the Dragon King.

So the Sea God's daughter became the bride of Urashima; and it was a bridal of wondrous splendor; and in the Dragon Palace there was great rejoicing.

And each day for Urashima there were new wonders and new pleasures:—wonders of the deepest deep brought up by the servants of the Ocean God;—pleasures of that enchanted land where summer never dies. And so three years passed.

But in spite of all these things, the fisher-boy felt always a heaviness at his heart when he thought of his parents waiting alone. So that at last he prayed his bride to let him go home for a little while only, just to say one word to his father and mother,—after which he would hasten back to her.

At these words she began to weep; and for a long time she continued to weep silently. Then she said to him: "Since you wish to go, of course you must go. I fear your going very much; I fear we shall never see each other again. But I will give you a little box to take with you. It will help you to come back to me if you will do what I tell you. Do not open it. Above all things, do not open it,—no matter what may happen! Because, if you open it, you will never be able to come back, and you will never see me again."

Then she gave him a little lacquered box tied about with a silken cord. (And that box can be seen unto this day in the temple of Kanagawa, by the seashore; and the priests there also keep Urashima Taro's fishing-line, and some strange jewels which he brought back with him from the realm of the Dragon King.)

But Urashima comforted his bride, and promised her never, never to open the box—never even to loosen the silken string. Then he passed away through the summer light over the ever-sleeping sea;—and the shape of the island where summer never dies faded behind him like a dream;—and he saw again before him the blue mountains of Japan, sharpening in the white glow of the northern horizon.

Again at last he glided into his native bay;—again he stood upon its beach. But as he looked, there came upon him a great bewilderment,—a weird doubt.

For the place was at once the same, and yet not the same. The cottage of his fathers had disappeared. There was a village; but the shapes of the houses were all strange, and the fields, and even the faces of the people. Nearly all remembered landmarks were gone;—the Shinto temple appeared to have been rebuilt in a new place; the woods had vanished from the neighboring slopes. Only the voice of the little stream flowing through the settlement, and the forms of the mountains, were still the same. All else was unfamiliar and new. In vain he tried to find the dwelling of his parents; and the fisherfolk stared wonderingly at him; and he could not remember having ever seen any of those faces before.

There came along a very old man, leaning on a stick, and Urashima asked him the way to the house of the Urashima family. But the old man looked quite astonished, and made him repeat the question many times, and then cried out:—

"Urashima Taro! Where do you come from that you do not know the story? Urashima Taro! Why, it is more than four hundred years since he was drowned, and a monument is erected to his memory in the graveyard. The graves of all his people are in that graveyard,—the old graveyard which is not used any more. Urashima Taro! How can you be so foolish as to ask where his house is?" And the old man hobbled on, laughing at the simplicity of his questioner.

But Urashima went to the village graveyard,—the old graveyard that was not used any more,—and there he found his own tombstone, and the tombstones of his father and his mother and his kindred, and the tombstones of many others he had known. So old were they, so moss-eaten, that it was very hard to read the names upon them.

Then he knew himself the victim of some strange illusion, and he took his way back to the beach,— always carrying in his hand the box, the gift of the Sea God's daughter. But what was this illusion? And what could be in that box? Or might not that which was in the box be the cause of the illusion? Doubt mastered faith. Recklessly he broke the promise made to his beloved;—he loosened the silken cord;—he opened the box!

Instantly, without any sound, there burst from it a white spectral vapor that rose in the air like a summer cloud, and began to drift away swiftly into the south, over the silent sea. There was nothing else in the box.

And Urashima then knew that he had destroyed his own happiness,—that he could never again return to his beloved, the daughter of the Ocean King. So that he wept and cried out bitterly in his despair.

Yet for a moment only. In another, he himself was changed. An icy chill shot through all his blood;—his teeth fell out; his face shriveled; his hair turned white as snow; his limbs withered; his strength ebbed; he sank down lifeless on the sand, crushed by the weight of four hundred winters.

Now in the official annals of the Emperors it is written that "in the twenty-first year of the Mikado Yuriaku, the boy Urashima of Midzunoye, in the district of Yosa, in the province of Tango, a descendant of the divinity Shimanemi, went to Elysium (Horai) in a fishing-boat." After this there is no more news of Urashima during the reigns of thirty-one emperors and empresses—that is, from the fifth until the ninth century. And then the annals announce that "in the second year of Tenchiyo, in the reign of the Mikado Go-Junwa, the boy Urashima returned, and presently departed again, none knew whither."[1]

1. See *The Classical Poetry of the Japanese*, by Professor Chamberlain, in Trubner's *Oriental Series*. According to Western chronology, Urashima went fishing in 477 A.D. and returned in 825.

III

The fairy mistress came back to tell me that everything was ready, and tried to lift my valise in her slender hands,—which I prevented her from doing, because it was heavy. Then she laughed, but would not suffer that I should carry it myself, and summoned a sea-creature with Chinese characters upon his back. I made obeisance to her; and she prayed me to remember the unworthy house despite the rudeness of the maidens. "And you will pay the kurumaya," she said, "only seventy-five sen."

Then I slipped into the vehicle; and in a few minutes the little gray town had vanished behind a curve. I was rolling along a white road overlooking the shore. To the right were pale brown cliffs; to the left only space and sea.

Mile after mile I rolled along that shore, looking into the infinite light. All was steeped in blue,—a marvelous blue, like that which comes and goes in the heart of a great shell. Glowing blue sea met hollow blue sky in a brightness of electric fusion; and vast blue apparitions—the mountains of Higo—angled up through the blaze, like masses of amethyst. What a blue transparency! The universal color was broken only by the dazzling white of a few high summer clouds, motionlessly curled above one phantom peak in the offing. The threw down upon the water snowy tremulous lights. Midges of ships creeping far away seemed to pull long threads after them,—the only sharp lines in all that hazy glory. But what divine clouds! White purified spirits of clouds, resting on their way to the beatitude of Nirvana? Or perhaps the mists escaped from Urashima's box a thousand years ago?

The gnat of the soul of me flitted out into that dream of blue, 'twixt sea and sun,—hummed back to the shore of Suminoye through the luminous ghosts of fourteen hundred summers. Vaguely I felt beneath me the drifting of a keel. It was the time of the Mikado Yuriaku. And the daughter of the Dragon King said tinklingly,—"Now we will go to my father's palace where it is always blue." "Why always blue?" I asked. "Because," she said, "I put all the clouds into the Box." "But I must go home," I answered resolutely. "Then," she said, "you will pay the kuru-maya only seventy-five sen."

Wherewith I woke into Doyo, or the period of Greatest Heat, in the twenty-sixth year of Meiji—and saw proof of the era in a line of telegraph poles reaching out of sight on the land side of the way. The kuruma was still fleeing by the shore, before the same blue vision of sky, peak and sea; but the white clouds were gone!—and there were no more cliffs close to the road, but fields of rice and of barley stretching to far-off hills. The telegraph lines absorbed my attention for a moment, because on the top wire, and only on the top wire, hosts of little birds were perched, all with their heads to the road, and nowise disturbed by our coming. They remained quite still, looking down upon us as mere passing phenomena. There were hundreds and hundreds in rank, for miles and miles. And I could not see one having its tail turned to the road. Why they sat thus, and what they were watching or waiting for, I could not guess. At intervals I waved my hat and shouted, to startle the ranks. Whereupon a few would rise up fluttering and chippering, and drop back again upon the wire in the same position as before. The vast majority refused to take me seriously.

The sharp rattle of the wheels was drowned by a deep booming; and as we whirled past a village I caught sight of an immense drum under an open shed, beaten by naked men.

"O kurumaya!" I shouted—"that—what is it?"

He, without stopping, shouted back:—

"Everwhere now the same thing is. Much time-in rain has not been seen: so the gods-to prayers are made, and drums are beaten."

We flashed through other villages; and I saw and heard more drums of various sizes, and from hamlets invisible, over miles of parching rice-fields, yet other drums, like echoings, responded.

IV

Then I began to think about Urashima again. I thought of the pictures and poems and proverbs recording the influence of the legend upon the imagination of a race. I thought of an Izumo dancing-girl I saw at a banquet acting the part of Urashima, with a little lacquered box whence there issued at the tragical minute a mist of Kyoto incense. I thought about the antiquity of the beautiful dance,—and therefore about vanished generations of dancing-girls,—and therefore about dust in the abstract;

which, again, led me to think of dust in the concrete, as bestirred by the sandals of the kurumaya to whom I was to pay only seventy-five sen. And I wondered how much of it might be old human dust, and whether in the eternal order of things the motion of hearts might be of more consequence than the motion of dust. Then my ancestral morality took alarm; and I tried to persuade myself that a story that had lived for a thousand years, gaining fresher charm with the passing of every century, could only have survived by virtue of some truth in it. But what truth? For the time being I could find no answer to this question.

The heat had become very great; and I cried

"O kurumaya! the throat of Selfishness is dry; water desirable is."

He, still running, answered:—

"The Village of the Long Beach inside of—not far—a great gush-water is. There pure august water will be given."

I cried again:—

"O kurumaya!—those little birds as-for, why this way always facing?"

He, running still more swiftly, responded:—

"All birds wind-to facing sit."

I laughed first at my own simplicity; then at my forgetfulness,—remembering I had been told the same thing, somewhere or other, when a boy. Perhaps the mystery of Urashima might also have been created by forgetfulness.

I thought again about Urashima. I saw the Daughter of the Dragon King waiting vainly in the

palace made beautiful for his welcome,—and the piti-
less return of the Cloud, announcing what had happened,—and the loving uncouth sea-creatures, in
their garments of great ceremony, trying to comfort
her. But in the real story there was nothing of all
this; and the pity of the people seemed to be all for
Urashima. And I began to discourse with myself
thus:—

Is it right to pity Urashima at all? Of course he
was bewildered by the gods. But who is not bewildered by the gods? What is Life itself but a bewilderment? And Urashima in his bewilderment doubted
the purpose of the gods, and opened the box. Then
he died without any trouble, and the people built a
shrine to him as Urashima Mio-jin. Why, then, so
much pity?

Things are quite differently managed in the West.
After disobeying Western gods, we have still to remain alive and to learn the height and the depth of
superlative sorrow. We are not allowed to die quite
comfortably just at the best possible time: much less
are we suffered to become after death small gods in
our own right. How can we pity the folly of Urashima after he had lived so long alone with visible
gods.

Perhaps the fact that we do may answer the riddle.
This pity must be self-pity; wherefore the legend may
be the legend of a myriad souls. The thought of it
comes just at a particular time of blue light and soft
wind,—and always like an old reproach. It has too
intimate relation to a season and the feeling of a
season not to be also related to something real in

one's life, or in the lives of one's ancestors. But what was that real something? Who was the Daughter of the Dragon King? Where was the island of unending summer? And what was the cloud in the box?

I cannot answer all those questions. I know this only,—which is not at all new:—

I have memory of a place and a magical time in which the Sun and the Moon were larger and brighter than now. Whether it was of this life or of some life before I cannot tell. But I know the sky was very much more blue, and nearer to the world,—almost as it seems to become above the masts of a steamer steaming into equatorial summer. The sea was alive and used to talk,—and the Wind made me cry out for joy when it touched me. Once or twice during other years, in divine days lived among the peaks, I have dreamed just for a moment that the same wind was blowing,—but it was only a remembrance.

Also in that place the clouds were wonderful, and of colors for which there are no names at all,—colors that used to make me hungry and thirsty. I remember, too, that the days were ever so much longer than these days,—and that every day there were new wonders and new pleasures for me. And all that country and time were softly ruled by One who thought only of ways to make me happy. Sometimes I would refuse to be made happy, and that always caused her pain, although she was divine;—and I remember that I tried very hard to be sorry. When day was done, and there fell the great hush of the light before moonrise, she would tell me stories that made me tingle from head to foot with pleasure. I have never heard any other stories half so beautiful. And when the pleasure became too great, she would sing a weird little song which always brought sleep. At last there came a parting day; and she wept, and told me of a charm she had given that I must never, never lose, because it would keep me young, and give me power to return. But I never returned. And the years went; and one day I knew that I had lost the charm, and had become ridiculously old.

V

The Village of the Long Beach is at the foot of a green cliff near the road, and consists of a dozen thatched cottages clustered about a rocky pool, shaded by pines. The basin overflows with cold water, supplied by a stream that leaps straight from the heart of the cliff,—just as folks imagine that a poem ought to spring straight from the heart of a poet. It was evidently a favorite halting-place, judging by the number of kuruma and people resting. There were benches under the trees; and after having allayed thirst, I sat down to smoke and to look at the women washing clothes and the travelers refreshing themselves at the pool,—while my kurumaya stripped, and proceeded to dash buckets of cold water over his body. Then tea was brought me by a young man with a baby on his back; and I tried to play with the baby, which said "Ah, bah!"

Such are the first sounds uttered by a Japanese babe. But they are purely Oriental; and in Romaji should be written *Aba*. And, as an utterance untaught, *Aba* is interesting. It is in Japanese child-speech the word for "good-by,"—precisely the last we would expect an infant to pronounce on entering into this world of illusion. To whom or to what is the little soul saying good-by?—to friends in a previous state of existence still freshly remembered?—to comrades of its shadowy journey from nobody-knows-where? Such theorizing is tolerably safe, from a pious point of view, since the child can never decide for us. What its thoughts were at that mysterious moment of first speech, it will have forgotten long before it has become able to answer questions.

Unexpectedly, a queer recollection came to me,—resurrected, perhaps, by the sight of the young man with the baby,—perhaps by the song of the water in the cliff: the recollection of a story:—

Long, long ago there lived somewhere among the mountains a poor wood-cutter and his wife. They were very old, and had no children. Every day the husband went alone to the forest to cut wood, while the wife sat weaving at home.

One day the old man went farther into the wood than was his custom, to seek a certain kind of wood; and he suddenly found himself at the edge of a little spring he had never seen before. The water was strangely clear and cold, and he was thirsty; for the day was hot, and he had been working hard. So he doffed his great straw hat, knelt down and took a long drink. The water seemed to refresh him in a most extraordinary way. Then he caught sight of his own face in the spring, and started back. It was certainly his own face, but not at all as he was accustomed to see it in the old mirror at home. It was the face of a very young man! He could not believe his eyes. He put up both hands to his head, which had been quite bald only a moment before. It was covered with thick black hair. And his face had become smooth as a boy's; every wrinkle was gone. At the same moment he discovered himself full of new strength. He stared in astonishment at the limbs that had been so long withered by age; they were now shapely and hard with dense young muscle. Unknowingly he had drunk at the Fountain of Youth; and that draught had transformed him.

First he leaped high and shouted for joy; then he ran home faster than he had ever run before in his life. When he entered his house his wife was frightened,—because she took him for a stranger; and when he told her the wonder, she could not at once believe him. But after a long time he was able to convince her that the young man she now saw before her was really her husband; and he told her where the spring was, and asked her to go there with him.

Then she said: "You have become so handsome and so young that you cannot continue to love an old woman;—so I must drink some of that water immediately. But it will never do for both of us to be away from the house at the same time. Do you wait here while I go." And she ran to the woods all by herself.

She found the spring and knelt down, and began to drink. Oh! how cool and sweet that water was! She drank and drank and drank, and stopped for breath only to begin again.

Her husband waited for her impatiently; he expected to see her come back changed into a pretty slender girl. But she did not come back at all. He got anxious, shut up the house, and went to look for her.

When he reached the spring, he could not see her. He was just on the point of returning when he heard a little wail in the high grass near the spring. He searched there and discovered his wife's clothes and a baby,—a very small baby, perhaps six months old!

For the old woman had drunk too deeply of the magical water; she had drunk herself far beyond the time of youth into the period of speechless infancy.

He took the child up in his arms. It looked at him in a sad, wondering way. He carried it home,—murmuring to it,—thinking strange, melancholy thoughts.

In that hour, after my reverie about Urashima, the moral of this story seemed less satisfactory than in former time. Because by drinking too deeply of life we do not become young.

Naked and cool my kurumaya returned, and said that because of the heat he could not finish the promised run of twenty-five miles, but that he had found another runner to take me the rest of the way. For so much as he himself had done, he wanted fifty-five sen.

It was really very hot—more than 100° I afterwards learned; and far away there throbbed continually, like a pulsation of the heat itself, the sound of great drums beating for rain. And I thought of the Daughter of the Dragon King.

"Seventy-five sen, she told me," I observed;—"and that promised to be done has not been done. Nevertheless, seventy-five sen to you shall be given,—because I am afraid of the gods."

And behind a yet unwearied runner I fled into the enormous blaze—in the direction of the great drums.

A CONSERVATIVE

He was born in a city of the interior, the seat of a daimyo of three hundred thousand koku, where no foreigner had ever been. The yashiki of his father, a samurai of high rank, stood within the outer fortifications surrounding the prince's castle. It was a spacious yashiki; and behind it and around it were landscape gardens, one of which contained a small shrine of the god of armies. Forty years ago there were many such homes. To artist eyes the few still remaining seem like fairy palaces, and their gardens like dreams of the Buddhist paradise.

But sons of samurai were severely disciplined in those days; and the one of whom I write had little time for dreaming. The period of caresses was made painfully brief for him. Even before he was invested with his first *hakama,* or trousers,—a great ceremony in that epoch,—he was weaned as far as possible from tender influence, and taught to check the natural impulses of childish affection. Little comrades would ask him mockingly, "Do you still need milk?" if they saw him walking out with his mother, although he might love her in the house as demonstratively as he pleased, during the hours he could pass by her side. These were not many. All inactive pleasures were severely restricted by his discipline; and even comforts, except during illness, were not allowed him. Almost from the time he could speak he was enjoined to consider duty the guiding motive of life, self-control the first requisite of conduct, pain and death matters of no consequence in the selfish sense.

There was a grimmer side to this Spartan discipline, designed to cultivate a cold sternness never to be relaxed during youth, except in the screened intimacy of the home. The boys were inured to the sight of blood. They were taken to witness executions; they were expected to display no emotion; and they were obliged, on their return home, to quell any secret feeling of horror by eating plentifully of rice tinted blood-color by an admixture of salted plum juice. Even more difficult things might be demanded of a very young boy,—to go alone at midnight to the execution-ground, for example, and bring back a head in proof of courage. For the fear of the dead was held not less contemptible in a samurai than the fear of man. The samurai child was pledged to fear nothing. In all such tests, the demeanor exacted was perfect impassiveness; any swaggering would have been judged quite as harshly as any sign of cowardice.

As a boy grew up, he was obliged to find his pleasures chiefly in those bodily exercises which were the samurai's early and constant preparations for war,—archery and riding, wrestling and fencing. Playmates were found for him; but these were older youths, sons of retainers, chosen for ability to assist him in the practice of martial exercises. It was their duty also to teach him how to swim, to handle a boat, to develop his young muscles. Between such physical training and the study of the Chinese classics the greater part of each day was divided for him. His diet, though ample, was never dainty; his clothing, except in time of great ceremony, was light and coarse; and he was not allowed the use of fire merely to warm himself. While studying of winter mornings, if his hands became too cold to use the writing brush, he would be ordered to plunge them into icy water to restore the circulation; and if his feet were numbed by frost, he would be told to run about in the snow to make them warm. Still more rigid was his training in the special etiquette of the military class; and he was early made to know that the little sword in his girdle was neither an ornament nor a plaything. He was shown how to use it, how to take his own life at a moment's notice, without shrinking, whenever the code of his class might so order.

Also in the matter of religion, the training of a samurai boy was peculiar. He was educated to revere the ancient gods and the spirits of his ancestors; he was well schooled in the Chinese ethics; and he was taught something of Buddhist philosophy and faith. But he was likewise taught that hope of heaven and fear of hell were for the ignorant only; and that the superior man should be influenced in his conduct by nothing more selfish than the love of right for its own sake, and the recognition of duty as a universal law.

Gradually, as the period of boyhood ripened into youth, his conduct was less subjected to supervision. He was left more and more free to act upon his own judgment,—but with full knowledge that a mistake would not be forgotten; that a serious offense would never be fully condoned; and that a well-merited reprimand was more to be dreaded than death. On the other hand, there were few moral dangers against which to guard him. Professional vice was then strictly banished from many of the provincial castle-towns; and even so much of the non-moral side of life as might have been reflected in popular romance and drama, a young samurai could know little about. He was taught to despise that common literature appealing either to the softer emotions or the passions, as essentially unmanly reading; and the public theatre was forbidden to his class. Thus, in that innocent provincial life of Old Japan, a young samurai might grow up exceptionally pure-minded and simple-hearted.

So grew up the young samurai concerning whom these things are written,—fearless, courteous, self-denying, despising pleasure, and ready at an instant's notice to give his life for love, loyalty, or honor. But though already a warrior in frame and spirit, he was in years scarcely more than a boy when the country was first startled by the coming of the Black Ships.

II

The policy of Iyemitsu, forbidding any Japanese to leave the country under pain of death, had left the nation for two hundred years ignorant of the outer world. About the colossal forces gathering beyond seas nothing was known. The long existence of the Dutch settlement at Nagasaki had in no wise enlightened Japan as to her true position,—an Oriental feudalism of the sixteenth century menaced by a Western world three centuries older. Accounts of the real wonders of that world would have sounded to Japanese ears like stories invented to please children, or have been classed with ancient tales of the fabled palaces of Horai. The advent of the American fleet, "the Black Ships," as they were then called, first awakened the government to some knowledge of its own weakness, and of danger from afar.

National excitement at the news of the second coming of the Black Ships was followed by consternation at the discovery that the Shogunate confessed its inability to cope with the foreign powers. This could only mean a peril greater than that of the Tartar invasion in the days of Hojo Tokimune, when the people had prayed to the gods for help, and the Emperor himself, at Ise, had besought the spirits of his fathers. Those prayers had been answered by sudden darkness, a sea of thunder, and the coming of the mighty wind still called *Kami-kaze,*—"the Wind of the Gods," by which the fleets of Kublai Khan were given to the abyss. Why should not prayers now also be made? They were, in countless homes and at thousands of shrines. But the Superior Ones gave this time no answer; the Kami-kaze did not come. And the samurai boy, praying vainly before the little shrine of Hachiman in his father's garden, wondered if the gods had lost their power, or if the people of the Black Ships were under the protection of stronger gods.

III

It soon became evident that the foreign "barbarians" were not to be driven away. Hundreds had come, from the East as well as from the West; and all possible measures for their protection had been taken; and they had built queer cities of their own upon Japanese soil. The government had even commanded that Western knowledge was to be taught

in all schools; that the study of English was to be
made an important branch of public education; and
that public education itself was to be remodeled
upon Occidental lines. The government had also
declared that the future of the country would
depend upon the study and mastery of the languages
and the science of the foreigners. During the interval, then, between such study and its successful results, Japan would practically remain under alien
domination. The fact was not, indeed, publicly
stated in so many words; but the significance of the
policy was unmistakable. After the first violent
emotions provoked by knowledge of the situation,—
after the great dismay of the people, and the sup-
pressed fury of the samurai,—there arose an intense
curiosity regarding the appearance and character of
those insolent strangers who had been able to obtain
what they wanted by mere display of superior force.
This general curiosity was partly satisfied by an immense production and distribution of cheap colored
prints, picturing the manner and customs of the barbarians, and the extraordinary streets of their set-
tlements. Caricatures only those flaring wood-prints
could have seemed to foreign eyes. But caricature
was not the conscious object of the artist. He tried
to portray foreigners as he really saw them; and he
saw them as green-eyed monsters, with red hair
like Shojo,[1] and with noses like Tengu,[2] wearing
clothes of absurd forms and colors; and dwelling in
structures like storehouses or prisons. Sold by hun-

1. Apish mythological beings with red hair, delighting in drunkenness.
2. Mythological beings of several kinds, supposed to live in the
mountains. Some have long noses.

dreds of thousands throughout the interior, these prints must have created many uncanny ideas. Yet as attempts to depict the unfamiliar they were only innocent. One should be able to study those old drawings in order to comprehend just how we appeared to the Japanese of that era; how ugly, how grotesque, how ridiculous.

The young samurai of the town soon had the experience of seeing a real Western foreigner, a teacher hired for them by the prince. He was an Englishman. He came under the protection of an armed escort; and orders were given to treat him as a person of distinction. He did not seem quite so ugly as the foreigners in the Japanese prints: his hair was red, indeed, and his eyes of a strange color; but his face was not disagreeable. He at once became, and long remained, the subject of tireless observation. How closely his every act was watched could never be guessed by any one ignorant of the queer superstitions of the pre-Meiji era concerning ourselves. Although recognized as intelligent and formidable creatures, Occidentals were not generally regarded as quite human; they were thought of as more closely allied to animals than to mankind. They had hairy bodies of queer shape; their teeth were different from those of men; their internal organs were also peculiar; and their moral ideas those of goblins. The timidity which foreigners then inspired, not, indeed, to the samurai, but to the common people, was not a physical, but a superstitious fear. Even the Japanese peasant has never been a coward. But to know his feelings in that time toward foreigners, one must also know something of the ancient beliefs, common to both Japan and China, about animals gifted with supernatural powers, and capable of assuming human form; about the existence of races half-human and half-superman; and about the mythical beings of the old picture-books, — goblins long-legged and long-armed and bearded (*ashinaga* and *tenaga*), whether depicted by the illustrators of weird stories or comically treated by the brush of Hokusai. Really the aspect of the new strangers seemed to afford confirmation of the fables related by a certain Chinese Herodotus; and the clothing they wore might have been devised for the purpose of hiding what would prove them not human. So the new English teacher, blissfully ignorant of the fact, was studied surreptitiously, just as one might study a curious animal! Nevertheless, from his students he experienced only courtesy: they treated him by that Chinese code which ordains that "even the shadow of a teacher must not be trodden on." In any event it would have mattered little to samurai students whether their teachers were perfectly human or not, so long as he could teach. The hero Yoshitsune had been taught the art of the sword by a Tengu. Beings not human had proved themselves scholars and poets. But behind the never-lifted mask of delicate courtesy, the stranger's habits were minutely noted; and the ultimate judgment, based upon the comparison of such observation, was not altogether flattering. The teacher himself could never have imagined the comments made upon him by his two-sworded pupils; nor would it have increased his peace of mind, while overlooking compositions in the class-room, to have understood their conversation:—

"See the color of his flesh, how soft it is! To take off his head with a single blow would be very easy."

Once he was induced to try their mode of wrestling, just for fun, he supposed. But they really wanted to take his physical measure. He was not very highly estimated as an athlete.

"Strong arms he certainly has," one said. "But he does not know how to use his body while using his arms; and his loins are very weak. To break his back would not be difficult."

"I think," said another, "that it would be very easy to fight with foreigners."

"With swords it would be very easy," responded a third; "but they are more skilful that we in the use of guns and cannon."

"We can learn all that," said the first speaker. "When we have learned Western military matters, we need not care for Western soldiers."

"Foreigners," observed another, "are not hardy like we are. They soon tire, and they fear cold. All winter our teacher must have a great fire in his room. To stay there five minutes gives me the headache."

But for all that, the lads were kind to their teacher, and made him love them.

IV

Changes came as great earthquakes come, without warning: the transformation of daimyates into prefectures, the suppression of the military class, the reconstruction of the whole social system. These events filled the youth with sadness, although he felt no difficulty in transferring his allegiance from prince to emperor, and although the wealth of his family remained unimpaired by the shock. All this reconstruction told him of the greatness of the national danger, and announced the certain disappearance of the old high ideals, and of nearly all things loved. But he knew regret was vain. By self-transformation alone could the nation hope to save its independence; and the obvious duty of the patriot was to recognize necessity, and fitly prepare himself to play the man in the drama of the future.

In the samurai school he had learned much English, and he knew himself able to converse with Englishmen. He cut his long hair, put away his swords, and went to Yokohama that he might continue his study of the language under more favorable conditions. At Yokohama everything at first seemed to him both unfamiliar and repellent. Even the Japanese of the port had been changed by foreign contact: they were rude and rough; they acted and spoke as common people would not have dared to do in his native town. The foreigners themselves impressed him still more disagreeably: it was the period when new settlers could assume the tone of conquerors to the conquered, and when the life of the "open ports" was much less decorous than now. The new buildings of brick or stuccoed timber revived for him unpleasant memories of the Japanese colored pictures of foreign manners and customs; and he could not quickly banish the fancies of his boyhood concerning Occidentals. Reason, based on larger knowledge and experience, fully assured him what they really were; but to his emotional life the intimate sense of their kindred humanity still failed to come. Race-feeling is older than intellectual development; and the superstitions attaching to race-feeling are not easy to get rid of. His soldier-spirit, too, was stirred at times by ugly things heard or seen,—incidents that filled him with the hot impulse of his fathers to avenge a cowardice or to redress a wrong. But he learned to conquer his repulsions as obstacles to knowledge: it was the patriot's duty to study calmly the nature of his country's foes. He trained himself at last to observe the new life about him without prejudice,—its merits not less than its defects; its strength not less than its weakness. He found kindness; he found devotion to ideals,—ideals not his own, but which he knew how to respect because they exacted, like the religion of his ancestors, abnegation of many things.

Through such appreciation he learned to like and to trust an aged missionary entirely absorbed in the work of educating and proselytizing. The old man was especially anxious to convert this young samurai, in whom aptitudes of no common order were discernible; and he spared no pains to win the boy's confidence. He aided him in many ways, taught him something of French and German, of Greek and Latin, and placed entirely at his disposal a private library of considerable extent. The use of a foreign library, including works of history, philosophy, travel, and fiction, was not a privilege then easy for Japanese students to obtain. It was gratefully appreciated; and the owner of the library found no difficulty at a later day in persuading his favored and favorite pupil to read a part of the New Testament. The youth expressed surprise at finding among the doctrines of the "Evil Sect" ethical precepts like those of Confucius. To the old missionary he said: "This teaching is not new to us; but it is certainly very good. I shall study the book and think about it."

V

The study and the thinking were to lead the young man much further than he had thought possible. After the recognition of Christianity as a great religion came recognitions of another order, and various imaginings about the civilization of the races professing Christianity. It then seemed to many reflective Japanese, possibly even to the keen minds directing the national policy, that Japan was doomed to pass altogether under alien rule. There was hope, indeed; and while even the ghost of hope remained, the duty for all was plain. But the power that could be used against the Empire was irresistible. And studying the enormity of that power, the young Oriental could not but ask himself, with a wonder approaching awe, whence and how it had been gained. Could it, as his aged teacher averred, have some occult relation to a higher religion? Certainly the ancient Chinese philosophy, which declared the prosperity of peoples proportionate to their observance of celestial law and their obedience to the teaching of sages, countenanced such a theory. And if the superior force of Western civilization really indicated the superior character of Western ethics, was it not the plain duty of every patriot to follow that higher faith, and to strive for the conversion of the whole nation? A youth of that era, educated in Chinese wisdom, and necessarily ignorant of the history of social evolution in the West, could never have imagined that the very highest forms of material progress were developed chiefly through a merciless competition out of all harmony with Christian idealism, and at variance with every great system of ethics. Even to-day in the West unthinking millions imagine some divine connection between military power and Christian belief; and utterances are made in our pulpits implying divine justification for political robberies, and heavenly inspiration for the invention of high explosives. There still survives among us the superstition that races professing Christianity are divinely destined to rob or exterminate races holding other beliefs. Some men occasionally express their conviction that we still worship Thor and Odin,—the only difference being that Odin has become a mathematician, and that the Hammer Mjolnir is now worked by steam. But such persons are declared by the missionaries to be atheists and men of shameless lives.

Be this as it may, a time came when the young samurai resolved to proclaim himself a Christian, despite the opposition of his kindred. It was a bold step; but his early training had given him firmness; and he was not to be moved from his decision even by the sorrow of his parents. His rejection of the ancestral faith would signify more than temporary pain for him: it would mean disinheritance, the contempt of old comrades, loss of rank, and all the consequences of bitter poverty. But his samurai training had taught him to despise self. He saw what he believed to be his duty as a patriot and as a truthseeker; and he followed it without fear or regret.

VI

Those who hope to substitute their own Western creed in the room of one which they wreck by the aid of knowledge borrowed from modern science, do not imagine that the arguments used against the ancient faith can be used with equal force against the new. Unable himself to reach the higher levels of modern thought, the average missionary cannot foresee the result of his small teaching of science upon an Oriental mind naturally more powerful than his own. He is therefore astonished and shocked to discover that the more intelligent his pupil, the briefer the term of that pupil's Christianity. To destroy personal faith in a fine mind previously satisfied with Buddhist cosmogony, because innocent of science, is not extremely difficult. But to substitute, in the same mind, Western religious emotions for Oriental, Presbyterian or Baptist dogmatisms for Chinese and Buddhist ethics, is not possible. The psychological difficulties in the way are never recognized by our modern evangelists. In former ages, when the faith of the Jesuits and the friars was not less superstitious than the faith they strove to supplant, the same deep-lying obstacles existed; and the Spanish priest, even while accomplishing marvels by his immense sincerity and fiery zeal, must have felt that to fully realize his dream he would need the sword of the Spanish soldier. To-day the conditions are far less favorable for any work of conversion than they were in the sixteenth century. Education has been secularized and remodeled upon a scientific basis; our religions are being changed into mere social recognitions of ethical necessities; the functions of our clergy are gradually being transformed into those of a moral police; and the multitude of our church-spires proves no increase of our faith, but only the larger growth of our respect for conventions. Never can the conventions of the Occident become those of the Far East; and never will foreign missionaries be suffered in Japan to take the role of a police of morals. Already the most liberal of our churches, those of broadest culture, begin to recognize the vanity of missions. But it is not necessary to drop old dogmatisms in order to perceive the truth: thorough education should be enough to reveal it; and the most educated of nations, Germany, sends no missionaries to work in the interior of Japan. A result of missionary efforts, much more significant than the indispensable yearly report of new conversions, has been the reorganization of the native religions, and a recent government mandate insisting upon the higher education of the native priesthoods. Indeed, long before this mandate the wealthier sects had established Buddhist schools on the Western plan; and the Shinshu could already boast of its scholars, educated in Paris or at Oxford, —men whose names are known to Sanscritists the world over. Certainly Japan will need higher forms of faith than her mediaeval ones; but these must be themselves evolved from the ancient forms,—from within, never from without. A Buddhism strongly fortified by Western science will meet the future needs of the race.

The young convert at Yokohama proved a noteworthy example of missionary failures. Within a few years after having sacrificed a fortune in order to become a Christian,—or rather the member of a foreign religious sect,—he publicly renounced the creed accepted at such a cost. He had studied and comprehended the great minds of the age better than his religious teachers, who could no longer respond to the questions he propounded, except by the assurance that books of which they had recommended him to study parts were dangerous to faith as wholes. But as they could not prove the fallacies alleged to exist in such books, their warnings availed nothing. He had been converted to dogmatism by imperfect reasoning; by larger and deeper reasoning he found his way beyond dogmatism. He passed from the church after an open declaration that its tenets were not based upon true reason or fact; and that he felt himself obliged to accept the opinions of men whom his teachers had called the enemies of Christianity. There was great scandal at his "relapse."

The real "relapse" was yet far away. Unlike many with a similar experience, he knew that the religious question had only receded for him, and that all he had learned was scarcely more than the alphabet of what remained to learn. He had not lost belief in the relative value of creeds,—in the worth of religion as a conserving and restraining force. A distorted perception of one truth—the truth of a relation subsisting between civilizations and the religions—had first delude him into the path that led to his conversion. Chinese philosophy had taught him that which modern sociology recognizes in the law that societies without priesthoods have never developed; and Buddhism had taught him that even delusions—the parables, forms, and symbols presented as actualities to humble minds—have their value and their justification in aiding the development of human goodness. From such a point of view, Christianity had lost none of its interest for him; and though doubting what his teacher had told him about the superior morality of Christian nations, not at all illustrated in the life of the open ports, he desired to see for himself the influence of religion upon morals in the Occident; to visit European countries and to study the causes of their development and the reason of their power.

This he set out to do sooner than he had purposed. That intellectual quickening which had made him a doubter in religious matters had made him also a freethinker in politics. He brought down upon himself the wrath of the government by public expressions of opinion antagonistic to the policy of the hour; and, like others equally imprudent under the stimulus of new ideas, he was obliged to leave the country. Thus began for him a series of wanderings destined to carry him round the world. Korea first afforded him a refuge; then China, where he lived as a teacher; and at last he found himself on board a steamer bound for Marseilles. He had little money; but he did not ask himself how he was going to live in Europe. Young, tall, athletic, frugal and inured to hardship, he felt sure of himself; and he had letters to men abroad who could smooth his way.

But long years were to pass before he could see his native land again.

VII

During those years he saw Western civilization as few Japanese ever saw it; for he wandered through Europe and America, living in many cities, and toiling in many capacities,—sometimes with his brain, oftener with his hand,—and so was able to study the highest and the lowest, the best and the worst of the life about him. But he saw with the eyes of the Far East; and the ways of his judgments were not as our ways. For even as the Occidental regards the Far East, so does the Far East regard the Occidental,— only with this difference: that what each most esteems in itself is least likely to be esteemed by the other. And both are partly right and partly wrong; and there never had been, and never can be, perfect mutual comprehension.

Larger than all anticipation the West appeared to him,—a world of giants; and that which depresses even the boldest Occidental who finds himself, without means or friends, alone in a great city, must often have depressed the Oriental exile: that vague uneasiness aroused by the sense of being invisible to hurrying millions; by the ceaseless roar of traffic drowning voices; by monstrosities of architecture without a soul; by the dynamic display of wealth forcing mind and hand, as mere cheap machinery, to the uttermost limits of the possible. Perhaps he saw such cities as

Dore saw London: sullen majesty of arched glooms, and granite deeps beyond range of vision, and mountains of masonry with seas of labor in turmoil at their base, and monumental spaces displaying the grimness of ordered power slow-gathering through centuries. Of beauty there was nothing to make appeal to him between those endless cliffs of stone which walled out the sunrise and the sunset, the sky and the wind. All that which draws us to great cities repelled or oppressed him; even luminous Paris soon filled him with weariness. It was the first foreign city in which he made a long sojourn. French art, as reflecting the aesthetic thought of the most gifted of European races, surprised him much, but charmed him not at all. What surprised him especially were its studies of the nude, in which he recognized only an open confession of the one human weakness which, next to disloyalty or cowardice, his stoical training had taught him to most despise. Modern French literature gave him other reasons for astonishment. He could little comprehend the amazing art of the storyteller; the worth of the workmanship in itself was not visible to him; and if he could have been made to understand it as a European understands, he would have remained none the less convinced that such application of genius to production signified social depravity. And gradually, in the luxurious life of the capital itself, he found proof for the belief suggested to him by the art and the literature of the period. He visited the pleasure-resorts, the theatres, the opera; he saw with the eyes of an ascetic and a soldier, and wondered why the Western conception of the worth of life differed so little from the Far-Eastern conception of folly and of effeminacy. He saw fashionable balls, and exposures *de rigueur* intolerable to the Far-Eastern sense of modesty,—artistically calculated to suggest what would cause a Japanese woman to die of shame; and he wondered at criticisms he had heard about the natural, modest, healthy half-nudity of Japanese toiling under a summer sun. He saw cathedrals and churches in vast number, and near to them the palaces of vice, and establishments enriched by the stealthy sale of artistic obscenities. He listened to sermons by great preachers; and he heard blasphemies against all faith and love by priest-haters. He saw the circles of wealth, and the circles of poverty, and the abysses underlying both. The "restraining influence" of religion he did not see. That world had no faith. It was a world of mockery and masquerade and pleasure-seeking selfishness, ruled not by religion, but by police; a world into which it was not good that a man should be born.

England, more sombre, more imposing, more formidable, furnished him with other problems to consider. He studied her wealth, forever growing, and the nightmares of squalor forever multiplying in the shadow of it. He saw the vast ports gorged with the riches of a hundred lands, mostly plunder; and knew the English still like their forefathers, a race of prey; and thought of the fate of millions if she should find herself for even a single month unable to compel other races to feed them. He saw the harlotry and drunkenness that make night hideous in the world's greatest city; and he marveled at the conventional hypocrisy that pretends not to see, and at the religion that utters thanks for existing conditions, and at the ignorance that sends missionaries where they are not needed, and at the enormous charities that help disease and vice to propagate their kind. He saw also the declaration of a great Englishman who had traveled in many countries that one tenth of the population of England were professional criminals or paupers. And this in spite of the myriads of churches, and the incomparable multiplication of laws! Certainly English civilization showed less than any other the pretended power of that religion which he had been taught to believe the inspiration of progress. English streets told him another story: there were no such sights to be seen in the streets of Buddhist cities. No: this civilization signified a perpetual wicked struggle between the simple and the cunning, the feeble and the strong; force and craft combining to thrust weakness into a yawning and visible hell. Never in Japan had there been even the sick dream of such conditions. Yet the merely material and intellectual results of those conditions he could not but confess to be astonishing; and though he saw evil beyond all he could have imagined possible, he saw also much good, among both poor and rich. The stupendous riddle of it all, the countless contradictions, were above his powers of interpretation.

He liked the English people better than the people of other countries he had visited; and the manners of the English gentry impressed him as not unlike those of the Japanese samurai. Behind their formal coldness he could discern immense capacities of friendship and enduring kindness,—kindness he experienced more than once; the depth of emotional power rarely wasted; and the high courage that had won the dominion of half a world. But ere he left England for America, to study a still vaster field of human achievement, mere differences of nationality had ceased to interest him: they were blurred out of visibility in his growing perception of Occidental civilization as one amazing whole, everywhere displaying—whether through imperial, monarchical, or democratic forms—the working of the like merciless necessities with the like astounding results, and everywhere based on ideas totally the reverse of Far-Eastern ideas. Such civilization he could estimate only as one having no single emotion in harmony with it,—as one finding nothing to love while dwelling in its midst, and nothing to regret in the hour of leaving it forever. It was as far away from his soul as the life of another planet under another sun. But he could understand its cost in terms of human pain, feel the menace of its weight, and divine the prodigious range of its intellectual power. And he hated it,—hated its tremendous and perfectly calculated mechanism; hated its utilitarian stability; hated its conventions, its greed, its blind cruelty, its huge hypocrisy, the foulness of its want and the insolence of its wealth. Morally, it was monstrous; conventionally, it was brutal. Depths of degradation unfathomable it had shown him, but no ideals equal to the ideals of his youth. It was all one great wolfish struggle; and that so much real goodness as he found in it could exist, seemed to him scarcely less than miraculous. The real sublimities of the Occident were intellectual only; far steep cold heights of pure knowledge, below whose perpetual snow-line emotional ideas die. Surely the old Japanese civilization of benevolence and duty was incomparably better in its comprehension of happiness, in its moral ambitions, its larger faith, its joyous courage, its simplicity, its sobriety and contentment. Western superiority was *not* ethical. It lay in forces of intellect developed through suffering incalculable, and used for the destruction of the weak by the strong.

And, nevertheless, that Western science whose logic he knew to be irrefutable assured him of the larger and larger expansion of the power of that civilization, as of an irresistible, inevitable, measureless inundation of world-pain. Japan would have to learn the new forms of action, to master the new forms of thought, or to perish utterly. There was no other alternative. And then the doubt of all doubts came to him, the question which all the sages have had to face: *Is the universe moral?* To that question Buddhism had given the deepest answer.

But whether moral or immoral, as measured by infinitesimal human emotion, one conviction remained with him that no logic could impair: the certainty that man should pursue the highest moral ideal with all his power to the unknown end, even though the suns in their courses should fight against him. The necessities of Japan would oblige her to master foreign science, to adopt much from the material civilization of her enemies; but the same necessities could not compel her to cast bodily away her ideas of right and wrong, of duty and of honor. Slowly a purpose shaped itself in his mind,—a purpose which was to make him in after years a leader and a teacher: to strive with all his strength for the conservation of all that was best in the ancient life, and to fearlessly oppose further introduction of anything not essential to national self-preservation, or helpful to national self-development. Fail he well might, and without shame; but he could hope at least to save something of worth from the drift of wreckage. The wastefulness of Western life had impressed him more than its greed of pleasure and its capacity for pain: in the clean poverty of his own land he saw strength; in her unselfish thrift, the sole chance of competing with the Occident. Foreign civilization had taught him to understand, as he could never otherwise have understood, the worth and beauty of his own; and he longed for the hour of permission to return to the country of his birth.

VIII

It was through the transparent darkness of a cloudless April morning, a little before sunrise, that he saw again the mountains of his native land,—far lofty sharpening sierras, towering violet-black out of the circle of an inky sea. Behind the steamer which was bearing him back from exile the horizon was slowly filling with rosy flame. There were some foreigners already on the deck, eager to obtain the first and fairest view of Fuji from the Pacific;—for the first sight of Fuji at dawn is not to be forgotten in this life or the next. They watched the long procession of the ranges, and looked over the jagged looming into the deep night, where stars were faintly burning still,— and they could not see Fuji. "Ah!" laughed an officer they questioned, "you are looking too low! higher up—much higher!" Then they looked up, up, up into the heart of the sky, and saw the mighty summit pinkening like a wondrous phantom lotos-bud in the flush of the coming day: a spectacle that smote them dumb. Swiftly the eternal snow yellowed into gold, then whitened as the sun reached out beams to it over the curve of the world, over the shadowy ranges, over the very stars, it seemed; for the giant base remained viewless. And the night fled utterly; and soft blue light bathed all the hollow heaven; and colors awoke from sleep;—and before the gazers there opened the luminous bay of Yoko-hama, with the sacred peak, its base ever invisible, hanging above all like a snowy ghost in the arch of the infinite day.

Still in the wanderer's ears the words rang, *"Ah! you are looking too low!—higher up—much high-er!"*—making vague rhythm with an immense, ir-resistible emotion swelling at his heart. Then every-thing dimmed: he saw neither Fuji above, nor the nearing hills below, changing their vapory blue to green; nor the crowding of the ships in the bay; nor anything of the modern Japan; he saw the Old. The land-wind, delicately scented with odors of spring, rushed to him, touched his blood, and startled from long-closed cells of memory the shades of all that he had once abandoned and striven to forget. He saw the faces of his dead: he knew their voices over the graves of the years. Again he was a very little boy in his father's yashiki, wandering from luminous room to room, playing in sunned places where leaf-shadows trembled on the matting, or gazing into the soft green dreamy peace of the landscape garden.

Once more he felt the light touch of his mother's hand guiding his little steps to the place of morning worship, before the household shrine, before the tablets of the ancestors; and the lips of the man murmured again, with sudden new-found meaning, the simple prayer of the child.

SOME THOUGHTS ABOUT ANCESTOR-WORSHIP

For twelve leagues, Ananda, around the Sala-Grove, there is no spot in size even as the pricking of the point of the tip of a hair, which is not pervaded by powerful spirits. — THE BOOK OF THE GREAT DECEASE.

I

The truth that ancestor-worship, in various unobtrusive forms, still survives in some of the most highly civilized countries of Europe, is not so widely known as to preclude the idea that any non-Aryan race actually practising so primitive a cult must necessarily remain in the primitive stage of religious thought. Critics of Japan have pronounced this hasty judgment; and have professed themselves unable to reconcile the facts of her scientific progress, and the success of her advanced educational system, with the continuance of her ancestor-worship. How can the beliefs of Shinto coexist with the knowledge of modern science? How can the men who win distinction as scientific specialists still repect the household shrine or do reverence before the Shinto parish-temple? Can all this mean more than the ordered conservation of forms after the departure of faith? Is it not certain that with the further progress of education, Shinto, even as ceremonialism, must cease to exist?

Those who put such questions appear to forget that similar questions might be asked about the continuance of any Western faith, and similar doubts expressed as to the possibility of its survival for another century. Really the doctrines of Shinto are not in the least degree more irreconcilable with modern science than are the doctrines of Orthodox Christianity. Examined with perfect impartiality, I would even venture to say that they are less irreconcilable in more respects than one. They conflict less with our human ideas of justice; and, like the Buddhist doctrine of karma, they offer some very striking analogies with the scientific facts of heredity,—analogies which prove Shinto to contain an element of truth as profound as any single element of truth in any of the world's great religions. Stated in the simplest possible form, the peculiar element of truth in Shinto is the belief that the world of the living is directly governed by the world of the dead.

That every impulse or act of man is the work of a god, and that all the dead become gods, are the basic ideas of the cult. It must be remembered, however, that the term Kami, although translated by the term deity, divinity, or god, has really no such meaning as that which belongs to the English words: it has not even the meaning of those words as referring to the antique beliefs of Greece and Rome. It signifies that which is "above," "superior," "upper," "eminent," in the non-religious sense; in the religious sense it signifies a human spirit having obtained supernatural power after death. The dead are the "powers above," the "upper ones,"—the Kami. We have here a conception resembling very strongly the modern Spiritualistic notion of ghosts,—only that the Shinto idea is in no true sense democratic. The Kami are ghosts of greatly varying dignity and power,—belonging to spiritual hierarchies like the hierarchies of ancient Japanese society. Although essentially superior to the living in certain respects, the living are, nevertheless, able to give them pleasure or displeasure, to gratify or to offend them,—even sometimes to ameliorate their spiritual condition. Wherefore posthumous honors are never mockeries, but realities to the Japanese mind. During the present year,[1] for example, several distinguished statesmen and soldiers were raised to higher rank immediately after their death; and I read only the other day, in the official gazette, that "His Majesty has been pleased to posthumously confer the Second Class of the Order of the Rising Sun upon Major-General Baron Yamane, who lately died in Formosa." Such imperial acts must not be regarded only as formalities intended to honor the memory of brave and patriotic men; neither should they be thought of as intended merely to confer distinction upon the family of the dead. They are essentially of Shinto, and exemplify that intimate sense of relation between the visible and invisible worlds which is the special religious characteristic of Japan among all civilized countries. To Japanese thought the dead are not less real than the living. They take part in the daily life of the people, — sharing the humblest sorrows and the humblest joys. They attend the family repasts, watch over the well-being of the household, assist and rejoice in the prosperity of their descendants. They are present at the public pageants,

---

1. Written in September, 1895.

at all the sacred festivals of Shinto, at the military games, and at all the entertainments especially provided for them. And they are universally thought of as finding pleasure in the offerings made to them or the honors conferred upon them.

For the purpose of this little essay, it will be sufficient to consider the Kami as the spirits of the dead,—without making any attempt to distinguish such Kami from those primal deities believed to have created the land. With this general interpretation of the term Kami, we return, then, to the great Shinto idea that all the dead still dwell in the world and rule it; influencing not only the thoughts and the acts of men, but the conditions of nature. "They direct," wrote Motowori, "the changes of the seasons, the wind and the rain, the good and the bad fortunes of states and of individual men." They are, in short, the viewless forces behind all phenomena.

II

The most interesting sub-theory of this ancient spiritualism is that which explains the impulses and acts of men as due to the influence of the dead. The hypothesis no modern thinker can declare irrational, since it can claim justification from the scientific doctrine of psychological evolution, according to which each living brain represents the structural work of innumerable dead lives,—each character a more or less imperfectly balanced sum of countless dead experiences with good and evil. Unless we deny psychological heredity, we cannot honestly deny that our impulses and feelings, and the higher capacities evolved through the feelings, have literally been shaped by the dead, and bequeathed to us by the dead; and even that the general direction of our mental activities has been determined by the power of the special tendencies bequeathed to us. In such a sense the dead are indeed our Kami; and all our actions are truly influenced by them. Figuratively we may say that every mind is a world of ghosts,— ghosts incomparably more numerous than the acknowledged millions of the higher Shinto Kami; and that the spectral population of one grain of brain-matter more than realizes the wildest fancies of the mediaeval schoolmen about the number of angels able to stand on the point of a needle. Scientifically we know that within one tiny living cell may be stored up the whole life of a race,—the sum of all the past sensation of millions of years; perhaps even (who knows?) of millions of dead planets.

But devils would not be inferior to angels in the mere power of congregating upon the point of a needle. What of bad men and of bad acts in this theory of Shinto? Motowori made answer: "Whenever anything goes wrong in the world, it is to be attributed to the action of evil gods called the Gods of Crookedness, whose power is so great that the Sun-Goddess and the Creator-God are sometimes powerless to restrain them; much less are human beings always able to resist their influence. The prosperity of the wicked, and the misfortunes of the good, which seem opposed to ordinary justice, are thus explained." All bad acts are due to the influence of evil deities; and evil men may become evil Kami. There are no self-contradictions in this simplest of cults,—nothing complicated or hard to be understood. It is not certain that all men guilty of bad actions necessarily become "gods of crookedness," for reasons hereafter to be seen; but all men, good or bad, become Kami, or influences. And all evil acts are the results of evil influences.

Now this teaching is in accord with certain facts of heredity. Our best faculties are certainly bequests from the best of our ancestors; our evil qualities are inherited from natures in which evil, or that which we now call evil, once predominated. The ethical knowledge evolved within us by civilization demands that we strengthen the high powers bequeathed us by the best experience of our dead, and diminish the force of the baser tendencies we inherit. We are under obligation to reverence and to obey our good Kami, and to strive against our gods of crookedness. The knowledge of the existence of both is old as human reason. In some form or other, the doctrine of evil and of good spirits in personal attendance upon every soul is common to most of the great religions. Our own mediaeval faith developed the idea to a degree which must leave an impress on our language for all time; yet the faith in guardian angels and tempting demons evolutionally represents only the development of a cult once simple as the religion of the Kami. And this theory of mediaeval faith is likewise pregnant with truth. The white-winged form that whispered good into the right ear, the black shape that murmured evil into the left, do not indeed walk beside the man of the nineteenth century, but they dwell within his brain; and he knows their voices and feels their urging as well and as often as did his ancestors of the Middle Ages.

The modern ethical objection to Shinto is that both good and evil Kami are to be respected. "Just as the Mikado worshiped the gods of heaven and of earth, so his people prayed to the good gods in order to obtain blessings, and performed rites in honor of the bad gods to avert their displeasure. . . . As there are bad as well as good gods, it is necessary to propitiate them with offerings of agreeable food, with the playing of harps and the blowing of flutes, with singing and dancing, and with whatever else is likely to put them in good humor."[1] As a matter of fact, in modern Japan, the evil Kami appear to receive few offerings or honors, notwithstanding this express declaration that they are to be propitiated. But it will now be obvious why the early missionaries characterized such a cult as devil-worship,—although, to Shinto imagination, the idea of a devil, in the Western meaning of the word, never took shape. The seeming weakness of the doctrine is in the teaching that evil spirits are not to be warred upon,—a teaching essentially repellent to Roman Catholic feeling. But between the evil spirits of Christian and of Shinto belief there is a vast difference. The evil Kami is only the ghost of a dead man, and is not believed to be altogether evil,—since propitiation is possible. The conception of absolute, unmixed evil is not of the Far East. Absolute evil is certainly foreign to human nature, and therefore impossible in human ghosts. The evil Kami are not devils. They are simply ghosts, who influence the passions of men; and

1. Motowori, translated by Satow.

only in this sense the deities of the passions. Now Shinto is of all the religions the most natural, and therefore in certain respects the most rational. It does not consider the passions necessarily evil in themselves, but evil only according to cause, conditions, and degrees of their indulgence. Being ghosts, the gods are altogether human,—having the various good and bad qualities of men in varying proportions. The majority are good, and the sum of the influence of all is toward good rather than evil. To appreciate the rationality of this view requires a tolerably high opinion of mankind,—such an opinion as the conditions of the old society of Japan might have justified. No pessimist could profess pure Shintoism. The doctrine is optimistic; and whoever has a generous faith in humanity will have no fault to find with the absence of the idea of implacable evil from its teaching.

Now it is just in the recognition of the necessity for propitiating the evil ghosts that the ethically rational character of Shinto reveals itself. Ancient experience and modern knowledge unite in warning us against the deadly error of trying to extirpate or to paralyze certain tendencies in human nature,— tendencies which, if morbidly cultivated or freed from all restraint, lead to folly, to crime, and to countless social evils. The animal passions, the ape-and-tiger impulses, antedate human society, and are the accessories to nearly all crimes committed against it. But they cannot be killed; and they cannot be safely starved. Any attempt to extirpate them would signify also an effort to destroy some of the very highest emotional faculties with which they remain inseparably blended. The primitive impulses cannot even be numbed save at the cost of intellectual and emotional powers which give to human life all its beauty and all its tendencies, but which are, nevertheless, deeply rooted in the archaic soil of passion. The highest in us had its beginnings in the lowest. Asceticism, by warring against the natural feelings, has created monsters. Theological legislation, irrationally directed against human weaknesses, has only aggravated social disorders; and laws against pleasure have only provoked debaucheries. The history of morals teaches very plainly indeed that our bad Kami require some propitiation. The passions still remain more powerful than the reason in man, because they are incomparably older,—because they were once all-essential to self-preservation,—because they made that primal stratum of consciousness out of which the nobler sentiments have slowly grown. Never can they be suffered to rule; but woe to whoever would deny their immemorial rights!

III

Out of these primitive, but—as may now be perceived—not irrational beliefs about the dead, there have been evolved moral sentiments unknown to Western civilization. These are well worth considering, as they will prove in harmony with the most advanced conception of ethics,—and especially with that immense though yet indefinite expansion of the sense of duty which has followed upon the understanding of evolution. I do not know that we have any reason to congratulate ourselves upon the absence from our lives of the sentiments in question;—

I am even inclined to think that we may yet find it morally necessary to cultivate sentiments of the same kind. One of the surprises of our future will certainly be a return to beliefs and ideas long ago abandoned upon the mere assumption that they contained no truth,—beliefs still called barbarous, pagan, mediaeval, by those who condemn them out of traditional habit. Year after year the researches of science afford us new proof that the savage, the barbarian, the idolater, the monk, each and all have arrived, by different paths, as near to some one point of eternal truth as any thinker of the nineteenth century. We are now learning, also, that the theories of the astrologers and of the alchemists were but partially, not totally wrong. We have reason even to suppose that no dream of the invisible world has ever been dreamed,—that no hypothesis of the unseen has ever been imagined,—which future science will not prove to have contained some germ of reality.

Foremost among the moral sentiments of Shinto is that of loving gratitude to the past,—a sentiment having no real correspondence in our own emotional life. We know our past better than the Japanese know theirs;—we have myriads of books recording or considering its every incident and condition: but we cannot in any sense be said to love it or to feel grateful to it. Critical recognitions of its merits and of its defects;—some rare enthusiasms excited by its beauties; many strong denunciations of its mistakes: these represent the sum of our thoughts and feelings about it. The attitude of our scholarship in reviewing it is necessarily cold; that of our art, often more than generous; that of our religion, condemnatory for the most part. Whatever the point of view from which we study it, our attention is mainly directed to the work of the dead,—either the visible work that makes our hearts beat a little faster than usual while looking at it, or the results of their thoughts and deeds in relation to the society of their time. Of past humanity as unity,—of the millions long-buried as real kindred,—we either think not at all, or think only with the same sort of curiosity that we give to the subject of extinct races. We do indeed find interest in the record of some individual lives that have left large marks in history;—our emotions are stirred by the memories of great captains, statesmen, discoverers, reformers,—but only because the magnitude of that which they accomplished appeals to our own ambitions, desires, egotisms, and not at all to our altruistic sentiments in ninety-nine cases out of a hundred. The nameless dead to whom we owe most we do not trouble ourselves about,—we feel no gratitude, no love to them. We find it difficult to persuade ourselves that the love of ancestors can possibly be a real, powerful, penetrating, life-moulding, religious emotion in any form of human society,—which it certainly is in Japan. The mere idea is utterly foreign to our ways of thinking, feeling, acting. A partial reason for this, of course, is that we have no common faith in the existence of an actual spiritual relation between our ancestors and ourselves. If we happen to be irreligious, we do not believe in ghosts. If we are profoundly religious, we think of the dead as removed from us by judgment,—as absolutely separated from us during the period of our lives. It is true that among the peasantry of Roman Catholic countries there still exists a belief that the dead are permitted to return to earth once a year,—on the night of All Souls. But even according to this belief they are not considered as related to the living by any stronger bond than memory; and they are thought of,—as our collections of folk-lore bear witness,—rather with fear than love.

In Japan the feeling toward the dead is utterly different. It is a feeling of grateful and reverential love. It is probably the most profound and powerful of the emotions of the race,—that which especially directs national life and shapes national character. Patriotism belongs to it. Filial piety depends upon it. Family love is rooted in it. Loyalty is based upon it. The soldier who, to make a path for his comrades through the battle, deliberately flings away his life with a shout of *"Teikoku manzai!"*—the son or daughter who unmurmuring sacrifices all the happiness of existence for the sake, perhaps, of an undeserving or even cruel parent; the partisan who gives up friends, family, and fortune, rather than break the verbal promise made in other years to a now poverty-stricken master; the wife who ceremoniously robes herself in white, utters a prayer, and thrusts a sword into her throat to atone for a wrong done to strangers by her husband,—all these obey the will and hear the approval of invisible witnesses. Even among the skeptical students of the new generation, this feeling survives many wrecks of faith, and the old sentiments are still uttered: "Never must we cause shame to our ancestors;" "it is our duty to give honor to our ancestors." During my former engagement as a teacher of English, it happened more than once that ignorance of the real meaning behind such phrases prompted me to change them in written composition. I would suggest, for example, that the expression, "to do honor *to the memory of* our ancestors," was more correct than the phrase given. I remember one day even attempting to explain why we ought not to speak of ancestors exactly as if they were living parents! Perhaps my pupils suspected me of trying to meddle with their beliefs; for the Japanese never think of an ancestor as having become "only a memory": their dead are alive.

Were there suddenly to arise within us the absolute certainty that our dead are still with us,—seeing every act, knowing our every thought, hearing each word we utter, able to feel sympathy with us or anger against us, able to help us and delighted to receive our help, able to love us and greatly needing our love,—it is quite certain that our conceptions of life and duty would be vastly changed. We should have to recognize our obligations to the past in a very solemn way. Now, with the man of the Far East, the constant presence of the dead has been a matter of conviction for thousands of years: he speaks to them daily; he tries to give them happiness; and, unless a professional criminal, he never quite forgets his duty towards them. No one, says Hirata, who constantly discharges that duty, will ever be disrespectful to the gods or to his living parents. "Such a man will also be loyal to his friends, and kind and gentle with his wife and children; for the essence of this devotion is in true filial piety." And it is in this sentiment that

the secret of much strange feeling in Japanese character must be sought. Far more foreign to our world
of sentiment than the splendid courage with which
death is faced, or the equanimity with which the most
trying sacrifices are made, is the simple deep emotion
of the boy who, in the presence of a Shinto shrine
never seen before, suddenly feels the tears spring to
his eyes. He is conscious in that moment of what we
never emotionally recognize,—the prodigious debt of
the present to the past, and the duty of love to the
dead.

IV

If we think a little about our position as debtors,
and our way of accepting that position, one striking
difference between Western and Far-Eastern moral
sentiment will become manifest.

There is nothing more awful than the mere fact of
life as mystery when that fact first rushes fully into
consciousness. Out of unknown darkness we rise a
moment into sunlight, look about us, rejoice and
suffer, pass on the vibration of our being to other
beings, and fall back again into darkness. So a wave
rises, catches the light, transmits its motion, and sinks
back into sea. So a plant ascends from clay, unfolds
its leaves to light and air, flowers, seeds, and becomes
clay again. Only, the wave has no knowledge; the
plant has no perceptions. Each human life seems no
more than a parabolic curve of motion out of earth
and back to earth; but in that brief interval of change
it perceives the universe. The awfulness of the phe-

nomenon is that nobody knows anything about it. No mortal can explain this most common, yet most incomprehensible of all facts,—life in itself; yet every mortal who can think has been obliged betimes to think about it in relation to self.

I come out of mystery;—I see the sky and the land, men and women and their works; and I know that I must return to mystery;—and merely what this means not even the greatest of philosophers—not even Mr. Herbert Spencer—can tell me. We are all of us riddles to ourselves and riddles to each other; and space and motion and time are riddles; and matter is a riddle. About the before and the after neither the new-born nor the dead have any message for us. The child is dumb; the skull only grins. Nature has no consolation for us. Out of her formlessness issue forms which return to formlessness,—that is all. The plant becomes clay; the clay becomes a plant. When the plant turns to clay, what becomes of the vibration which was its life? Does it go on existing viewlessly, like the forces that shape spectres of frondage in the frost upon a window-pane?

Within the horizon-circle of the infinite enigma, countless lesser enigmas, old as the world, awaited the coming of man. Oedipus had to face one Sphinx; humanity, thousands of thousands,—all crouching among bones along the path of Time, and each with a deeper and a harder riddle. All the sphinxes have not been satisfied; myriads line the way of the future to devour lives yet unborn; but millions have been answered. We are now able to exist without perpetual horror because of the relative knowledge that guides us,—the knowledge won out of the jaws of destruction.

All our knowledge is bequeathed knowledge. The dead have left us record of all they were able to learn about themselves and the world,—about the laws of death and life,—about things to be acquired and things to be avoided,—about ways of making existence less painful than Nature willed it,—about right and wrong and sorrow and happiness,—about the error of selfishness, the wisdom of kindness, the obligation of sacrifice. They left us information of everything they could find out concerning climates and seasons and places,—the sun and moon and stars,— the motions and the composition of the universe. They bequeathed us also their delusions which long served the good purpose of saving us from falling into greater ones. They left us the story of their errors and efforts, their triumphs and failures, their pains and joys, their loves and hates,—for warning or example. They expected our sympathy, because they toiled with the kindest wishes and hopes for us, and because they made our world. They cleared the land; they extirpated monsters; they tamed and taught the animals most useful to us. *"The mother of Kullervo awoke within her tomb, and from the deeps of the dust she cried to him,—'I have left thee the Dog, tied to a tree, that thou mayest go with him to the chase.' "*[1] They domesticated likewise the useful trees and plants; and they discovered the places and the powers of the metals. Later they created all that we call civilization,—trusting us to correct such mistakes

---

1. *Kalevala;* thirty-sixth Rune.

as they could not help making. The sum of their toil is incalculable; and all that they have given us ought surely to be very sacred, very precious, if only by reason of the infinite pain and thought which it cost. Yet what Occidental dreams of saying daily, like the Shinto believer:—"*Ye forefathers of the generations, and of our families, and of our kindred,—unto you, the founders of our homes, we utter the gladness of our thanks*"?

None. It is not only because we think the dead cannot hear, but because we have not been trained for generations to exercise our powers of sympathetic mental representation except within a very narrow circle,—the family circle. The Occidental family is a very small affair indeed compared with the Oriental family circle. In this nineteenth century the Occidental family is almost disintegrated;—it practically means little more than husband, wife, and children well under age. The Oriental family means not only parents and their blood-kindred, but grandparents and their kindred, and great-grandparents, and all the dead behind them. The idea of the family cultivates sympathetic representation to such a degree that the range of emotion belonging to such representation may extend, as in Japan, to many groups and sub-groups of living families, and even, in time of national peril, to the whole nation as one great family: a feeling much deeper than what we call patriotism. As a religious emotion the feeling is infinitely extended to all the past; the blended sense of love, of loyalty, and of gratitude is not less real, though necessarily more vague, than the feeling to living kindred.

In the West, after the destruction of antique society, no such feeling could remain. The beliefs that
condemned the ancients to hell, and forbade the
praise of their works,—the doctrine that trained us
to return thanks for everything to the God of the
Hebrews,—created habits of thought and habits of
thoughtlessness, both inimical to every feeling of
gratitude to the past. Then, with the decay of theol-
ogy, came the teaching that the dead had no choice
in their work,—they had obeyed necessity, and we
had only received from them of necessity the results
of necessity. And to-day we still fail to recognize
that the necessity itself ought to compel our sym-
pathies with those who obeyed it, and that its bequeathed results are as pathetic as they are precious.
Such thoughts rarely occur to us even in regard to
the work of the living who serve us. We consider the
cost of a thing purchased or obtained to ourselves;
about its cost in effort to the producer we do not
allow ourselves to think: indeed, we should be
laughed at for any exhibition of conscience on the
subject. And our equal insensibility to the pathetic
meaning of the work of the past, and to that of the
work of the present, largely explains the wastefulness
of our civilization, — the reckless consumption by
luxury of the labor of years in the pleasure of an
hour,—the inhumanity of the thousands of unthinking rich, each of whom dissipates yearly in the gratification of totally unnecessary wants the price of a
hundred human lives. The cannibals of civilization
are unconsciously more cruel than those of savagery,
and require much more flesh. The deeper humanity,
—the cosmic emotion of humanity,—is essentially the

enemy of useless luxury, and essentially opposed to any form of society which places no restraints upon the gratification of sense or the pleasures of egotism.

In the Far East, on the other hand, the moral duty of simplicity of life has been taught from very ancient times, because ancestor-worship had developed and cultivated this cosmic emotion of humanity which we lack, but which we shall certainly be obliged to acquire at a later day, simply to save ourselves from extermination. Two sayings of Iyeyasu exemplify the Oriental sentiment. When virtually master of the empire, this greatest of Japanese soldiers and statesmen was seen one day cleaning and smoothing with his own hands an old dusty pair of silk hakama or trousers. "What you see me do," he said to a retainer, "I am not doing because I think of the worth of the garment in itself, but because I think of what it needed to produce it. It is the result of the toil of a poor woman; and that is why I value it. *If we do not think, while using things, of the time and effort required to make them,—then our want of consideration puts us on a level with the beasts.*" Again, in the days of his greatest wealth, we hear of him rebuking his wife for wishing to furnish him too often with new clothing. "When I think," he protested, "of the multitudes around me, and of the generations to come after me, I feel it my duty to be very sparing, for their sake, of the goods in my possession." Nor has this spirit of simplicity yet departed from Japan. Even the Emperor and the Empress, in the privacy of their own apartments, continue to live as simply as their subjects, and devote most of their revenue to the alleviation of public distress.

V

It is through the teachings of evolution that there will ultimately be developed in the West a moral recognition of duty to the past like that which ancestor-worship created in the Far East. For even to-day whoever has mastered the first principles of the new philosophy cannot look at the commonest product of man's handiwork without perceiving something of its evolutional history. The most ordinary utensil will appear to him, not the mere product of individual capacity on the part of carpenter or potter, smith or cutler, but the product of experiment continued through thousands of years with methods, with materials, and with forms. Nor will it be possible for him to consider the vast time and toil necessitated in the evolution of any mechanical appliance, and yet experience no generous sentiment. Coming generations *must* think of the material bequests of the past in relation to dead humanity.

But in the development of this "cosmic emotion" of humanity, a much more powerful factor than recognition of our material indebtedness to the past will be the recognition of our physical indebtedness. For we owe to the dead our immaterial world also,—the world that lives within us,—the world of all that is lovable in impulse, emotion, thought. Whosoever understands scientifically what human goodness is, and the terrible cost of making it, can find in the commonest phases of the humblest lives that beauty which is divine, and can feel that in one sense our dead are truly gods.

So long as we supposed the woman soul one in itself,—a something specially created to fit one particular physical being,—the beauty and the wonder of mother-love could never be fully revealed to us. But with deeper knowledge we must perceive that the inherited love of myriads of millions of dead mothers has been treasured up in one life;—that only thus can be interpreted the infinite sweetness of the speech which the infant hears,—the infinite tenderness of the look of caress which meets its gaze. Unhappy the mortal who has not known these; yet what mortal can adequately speak of them! Truly is mother-love divine; for everything by human recognition called divine is summed up in that love; and every woman uttering and transmitting its highest expression is more than the mother of man: she is the *Mater Dei*.

Needless to speak here about the ghostliness of first love, sexual love, which is illusion,—because the passion and the beauty of the dead revive in it, to dazzle, to delude, and to bewitch. It is very, very wonderful; but it is not all good, because it is not all true. The real charm of woman, in herself is that which comes later,—when all the illusions fade away to reveal a reality, lovelier than any illusion, which has been evolving behind the phantom-curtain of them. What is the divine magic of the woman thus perceived? Only the affection, the sweetness, the faith, the unselfishness, the institutions of millions of buried hearts. All live again;—all throb anew, in every fresh warm beat of her own.

Certain amazing faculties exhibited in the highest social life tell in another way the story of soul structure built by dead lives. Wonderful is the man who can really "be all things to all men," or the woman who can make herself twenty, fifty, a hundred different women,—comprehending all, penetrating all, unerring to estimate all others;—seeming to have no individual self, but only selves innumerable;—able to meet each varying personality with a soul exactly toned to the tone of that to be encountered. Rare these characters are, but not so rare that the traveler is unlikely to meet one or two of them in any cultivated society which he has a chance of studying. They are essentially multiple beings,—so visibly multiple that even those who think of the Ego as single have to describe them as "highly complex." Nevertheless this manifestation of forty or fifty different characters in the same person is a phenomemon so remarkable (especially remarkable because it is commonly manifested in youth long before relative experience could possibly account for it) that I cannot but wonder how few persons frankly realize its signification.

So likewise with what have been termed the "intuitions" of some form of genius,—particularly those which relate to the representation of the emotions. A Shakespeare would always remain incomprehensible on the ancient soul-theory. Taine attempted to explain him by the phrase, "a perfect imagination;"— and the phrase reaches far into the truth. But what is the meaning of a perfect imagination? Enormous multiplicity of soul-life,—countless past existences revived in one. Nothing else can explain it. . . . It is not, however, in the world of pure intellect that the story of psychical complexity is most admirable: it is in the world which speaks to our simplest emotions of love, honor, sympathy, heroism.

"But by such a theory," some critic may observe, "the source of impulses to heroism is also the source of the impulses that people jails. Both are of the dead." This is true. We inherited evil as well as good. Being composites only,—still evolving, still becoming,—we inherit imperfections. But the survival of the fittest in impulses is certainly proven by the average moral condition of humanity,—using the word "fittest" in its ethical sense. In spite of all the misery and vice and crime, nowhere so terribly developed as under our own so-called Christian civilization, the fact must be patent to any one who has lived much, traveled much, and thought much, that the mass of humanity is good, and therefore that the vast majority of impulses bequeathed us by past humanity is good. Also it is certain that the more normal a social condition, the better its humanity. Through all the past the good Kami have always managed to keep the bad Kami from controlling the world. And with the acceptation of this truth, our future ideas of wrong and of right must take immense expansion. Just as a heroism, or any act of pure goodness for a noble end, must assume a preciousness heretofore unsuspected,—so a real crime must come to be regarded as a crime less against the existing individual or society, than against the sum of human experience, and the whole past struggle of ethical aspiration. Real goodness will, therefore, be more prized, and real crime less leniently judged. And the early Shinto teaching, that no code of ethics is necessary,—that the right rule of human conduct can always be known by consulting the heart,—is a teaching which will doubtless be accepted by a more perfect humanity than that of the present.

VI

"Evolution," the reader may say, "does indeed show through its doctrine of heredity that the living are in one sense really controlled by the dead. But it also shows that the dead are within us, not without us. They are part of us;—there is no proof that they have any existence which is not our own. Gratitude to the past would, therefore, be gratitude to ourselves; love of the dead would be self-love. So that your attempt at analogy ends in the absurd."

No. Ancestor-worship in its primitive form may be a symbol only of truth. It may be an index or foreshadowing only of the new moral duty which larger knowledge must force upon us: the duty of reverence and obedience to the sacrificial past of human ethical experience. But it may also be much more. The facts of heredity can never afford but half an explanation of the facts of psychology. A plant produces ten, twenty, a hundred plants without yielding up its own life in the process. An animal gives birth to many young, yet lives on with all its physical capacities and its small powers of thought undiminished. Children are born; and parents survive them. Inherited the mental life certainly is, not less than the physical; yet the reproductive cells, the least specialized of all cells, whether in plant or in animal, never take away, but only repeat the parental being. Continually multiplying, each conveys and transmits the whole experience of a race; yet leaves the whole ex-experience of a race behind it. Here is the marvel inexplicable: the self-multiplication of physical and psychical being,—life after life thrown off from the parent life, each to become complete and reproductive. Were all the parent life given to the offspring, heredity might be said to favor the doctrine of materialism. But like the deities of Hindoo legend, the Self multiplies and still remains the same, with full capacities for continued multiplication. Shinto has its doctrine of souls multiplying by fission; but the facts of psychological emanation are infinitely more wonderful than any theory.

The great religions have recognized that heredity could not explain the whole question of self,—could not account for the fate of the original residual self. So they have generally united in holding the inner independent of the outer being. Science can no more fully decide the issues they have raised than it can decide the nature of Reality-in-itself. Again we may vainly ask, What becomes of the forces which constituted the vitality of a dead plant? Much more difficult the question, What becomes of the sensations which formed the psychical life of a dead man?—since no-body can explain the simplest sensation. We know only that during life certain active forces within the body of the plant or the body of the man adjusted themselves continually to outer forces; and that after the interior forces could no longer respond to the pressure of the exterior forces,—then the body in which the former were stored was dissolved into the elements out of which it had been built up. We know nothing more of the ultimate nature of those elements than we know of the ultimate nature of the tendencies which united them. But we have more right to believe the ultimates of life persist after the dissolution of the forms they created, than to believe they cease. The theory of spontaneous generation (mis-named, for only in a qualified sense can the term "spontaneous" be applied to the theory of the beginnings of mundane life) is a theory which the evolutionist must accept, and which can frighten none aware of the evidence of chemistry that matter itself is in evolution. The real theory (not the theory of organized life beginning in bottled infusions, but of the life primordial arising upon a planetary surface) has enormous—nay, infinite—spiritual significance. It requires the belief that all potentialities of life and thought and emotion pass from nebula to universe, from system to system, from star to planet or moon, and again back to cyclonic storms of atomicity; it means that tendencies survive sunburnings,—survive all cosmic evolutions and disintegrations. The elements are evolutionary products only; and the difference of universe from universe must be the creation of tendencies,—of a form of heredity too vast and complex for imagination. There is no chance. There is only law. Each fresh evolution must be influenced by previous evolutions,—just as each individual human life is influenced by the experience of all the lives in its ancestral chain. Must not the tendencies even of the ancestral forms of matter be inherited by the forms of matter to come; and may not the acts and thoughts of men even now be helping to shape the character of future worlds? No longer is it possible to say that the dreams of the Alchemists were absurdities. And no longer can we even assert that all material phenomena are not determined, as in the thought of the ancient East, by soul-polarities.

Whether our dead do or do not continue to dwell without us as well as within us,—a question not to be decided in our present undeveloped state of comparative blindness,—certain it is that the testimony of cosmic facts accords with one weird belief of Shinto: the belief that all things are determined by the dead,—whether by ghosts of men or ghosts of worlds. Even as our personal lives are ruled by the now viewless lives of the past, so doubtless the life of our Earth, and of the system to which it belongs, is ruled by ghosts of spheres innumerable: dead universes,—dead suns and planets and moons,—as forms long since dissolved into the night, but as forces immortal and eternally working.

Back to the Sun, indeed, like the Shintoist, we can trace our descent; yet we know that even there the beginning of us was not. Infinitely more remote in time than a million sun-lives was that begininng,— if it can truly be said there was a beginning.

The teaching of Evolution is that we are one with that unknown Ultimate, of which matter and human mind are but ever-changing manifestations. The teaching of Evolution is also that each of us is many, yet that all of us are one with each other and with the cosmos;—that we must know all past humanity not only in ourselves, but likewise in the preciousness and beauty of every fellow-life;—that we can best love ourselves in others;—that we shall best serve ourselves in others;—that forms are but veils and phantoms;—and that to the formless Infinite alone really belong all human emotions, whether of the living or the dead.

THE NUN OF THE TEMPLE OF AMIDA

When O-Toyo's husband—a distant cousin, adopted into her family for love's sake—had been summoned by his lord to the capital, she did not feel anxious about the future. She felt sad only. It was the first time since their bridal that they had ever been separated. But she had her father and mother to keep her company, and, dearer than either,—though she would never have confessed it even to herself,—her little son. Besides, she always had plenty to do. There were many household duties to perform, and there was much clothing to be woven—both silk and cotton.

Once daily at a fixed hour, she would set for the absent husband, in his favorite room, little repasts faultlessly served on dainty lacquered trays,—miniature meals such as are offered to the ghosts of the ancestors, and to the gods. These repasts were served at the east side of the room, and his kneeling-cushion placed before them. The reason they were served at the east side was because he had gone east. Before removing the food, she always lifted the cover of the little soup-bowl to see if there was any vapor upon its lacquered inside surface. For it is said that if there be vapor on the inside of the lid covering food so offered, the absent beloved is well. But if there be none, he is dead,—because that is a sign that his soul has returned by itself to seek nourishment. O-Toyo found the lacquer thickly beaded with vapor day by day.

The child was her constant delight. He was three years old, and fond of asking questions to which none but the gods know the real answers. When he wanted to play, she laid aside her work to play with him. When he wanted to rest, she told him wonderful stories, or gave pretty pious answers to his questions about those things which no man can ever understand. At evening, when the little lamps had been lighted before the holy tablets and the images, she taught his lips to shape the words of filial prayer. When he had been laid to sleep, she brought her work near to him, and watched the still sweetness of his face. Sometimes he would smile in his dreams; and she knew that Kwannon the divine was playing shadowy play with him, and she would murmur the Buddhist invocation to that Maid "who looketh forever down above the sound of prayer."

Sometimes, in the season of very clear days, she would climb the mountain of Dakeyama, carrying her little boy on her back. Such a trip delighted him much, not only because of what his mother taught him to see, but also of what she taught him to hear. The sloping way was through groves and woods, and over grassed slopes, and around queer rocks; and there were flowers with stories in their hearts, and trees holding tree-spirits. Pigeons cried *korup-korup;* and doves sobbed *owao, owao;* and cicadae wheezed and fluted and tinkled.

All those who wait for absent dear ones make, if they can, a pilgrimage to the peak called Dakeyama. It is visible from any part of the city; and from its summit several provinces can be seen. At the very top is a stone of almost human height and shape, perpendicularly set up; and little pebbles are heaped before it and upon it. And nearby there is a small Shinto shrine erected to the spirit of a princess of other days. For she mourned the absence of one she loved, and used to watch from this mountain for his coming until she pined away and was changed into a stone. The people therefore built the shrine; and lovers of the absent still pray there for the return of those dear to them; and each, after so praying, takes home one of the little pebbles heaped there. And when the beloved one returns, the pebble must be taken back to the pebble-pile upon the mountain-top, and other pebbles with it, for a thank-offering and commemoration.

Always ere O-Toyo and her son could reach their home after such a day, the dusk would fall softly about them; for the way was long, and they had to both go and return by boat through the wilderness of rice-fields round the town,—which is a slow manner of journeying. Sometimes stars and fireflies lighted them; sometimes also the moon, and O-Toyo would softly sing to her boy the Izumo child-song to the moon:—

> Nono-San,
> Little Lady Moon,
> How old are you?
> "Thirteen days,—
> Thirteen and nine."
> That is still young,
> And the reason must be

> For that bright red obi,
> So nicely tied,[1]
> And that nice white girdle
> About your hips.
> Will you give it to the horse?
>   "Oh, no, no!"
> Will you give it to the cow?
>   "Oh, no, no!"

And up to the blue night would rise from all those wet leagues of labored field that great soft bubbling chorus which seems the very voice of the soil itself,— the chant of the frogs. And O-Toyo would interpret its syllables to the child: *Me kayui! me kayui!* "Mine eyes tickle; I want to sleep."

All those were happy hours.

II

Then twice, within the time of three days, those masters of life and death whose ways belong to the eternal mysteries struck at her heart. First she was taught that the gentle husband for whom she had so often prayed never could return to her,—having been returned unto that dust out of which all forms are borrowed. And in another little while she knew her boy slept so deep a sleep that the Chinese physician could not waken him. These things she learned only as shapes are learned in lightning flashes. Between and beyond the flashes was that absolute darkness which is the pity of the gods.

---

1. Because an obi or girdle of very bright color can only be worn by children.

It passed; and she rose to meet a foe whose name is Memory. Before all others she could keep her face, as in other days, sweet and smiling. But when alone with this visitant, she found herself less strong. She would arrange little toys and spread out little dresses on the matting, and look at them, and talk to them in whispers, and smile silently. But the smile would ever end in a burst of wild, loud weeping; and she would beat her head upon the floor, and ask foolish questions of the gods.

One day she thought of a weird consolation—that rite the people name *Toritsu-banashi*,—the evocation of the dead. Could she not call back her boy for one brief moment only? It would trouble the little soul; but would he not gladly bear a moment's pain for her dear sake? Surely!

(To have the dead called back one must go to some priest—Buddhist or Shinto—who knows the rite of incantation. And the mortuary tablet, or ihai, of the dead must be brought to that priest.

Then ceremonies of purification are performed; candles are lighted and incense is kindled before the ihai; and prayers or parts of sutras are recited; and offerings of flowers and of rice are made. But, in this case, the rice must not be cooked.

And when everything has been made ready, the priest, taking in his left hand an instrument shaped like a bow, and striking it rapidly with his right, calls upon the name of the dead, and cries out the words, *kitazo yo! kitazo yo! kitazo yo!* meaning, "I have come." And, as he cries, the tone of his voice gradually changes until it becomes the very voice of the dead person,—for the ghost enters into him.

Then the dead will answer questions quickly asked, but will cry continually: "Hasten, hasten! for this my coming back is painful, and I have but a little time to stay!" And having answered, the ghost passes; and the priest falls senseless upon his face.

Now to call back the dead is not good. For by calling them back their condition is made worse. Returning to the underworld, they must take a lower place than that which they had held before.

To-day these rites are not allowed by law. They once consoled; but the law is a good law, and just,— since there exist men willing to mock the divine which is in human hearts.)

So it came to pass that O-Toyo found herself one night in a lonely little temple at the verge of the city,—kneeling before the ihai of her boy, and hearing the rite of incantation. And presently, out of the lips of the officiant there came a voice she thought she knew,—a voice loved above all others,—but faint and very thin, like a sobbing of wind.

And the thin voice cried to her:—

"Ask quickly, quickly, mother! Dark is the way and long; and I may not linger."

Then tremblingly she questioned:—

"Why must I sorrow for my child? What is the justice of the gods?"

And there was answer given:—

"O mother, do not mourn me thus! That I died was only that you might not die. For the year was a year of sickness and sorrow,—and it was given me to know that you were to die; and I obtained my prayer that I should take your place.

"O mother, never weep for me! It is not kindness to mourn for the dead. Over the River of Tears their silent road is; and when mothers weep, the flood of that river rises, and the soul cannot pass, but must wander to and fro.

"Therefore, I pray you, do not grieve, O mother mine! Only give me a little water sometimes."

III

From that hour she was not seen to weep. She performed, lightly and silently, as in former days, the gentle duties of a daughter.

Seasons passed; and her father thought to find another husband for her. To the mother he said:—

"If our daughter again have a son, it will be great joy for her, and for all of us."

But the wiser mother made answer:—

"Unhappy she is not. It is impossible that she marry again. She has become as a little child, knowing nothing of trouble or sin."

It was true that she had ceased to know real pain. She had begun to show a strange fondness for very small things. At first she had found her bed too large —perhaps through the sense of emptiness left by the loss of her child; then, day by day, other things seemed to grow too large,—the dwelling itself, the familiar rooms, the alcove and its great flower-vases, —even the household utensils. She wished to eat her rice with miniature chopsticks out of a very small bowl such as children use.

In these things she was lovingly humored; and in other matters she was not fantastic. The old people consulted together about her constantly. At last the father said:—

"For our daughter to live with strangers might be painful. But as we are aged, we may soon have to leave her. Perhaps we could provide for her by making her a nun. We might build a little temple for her."

Next day the mother asked O-Toyo:—

"Would you not like to become a holy nun, and to live in a very, very small temple, with a very small altar, and little images of the Buddhas? We should always be near you. If you wish this, we shall get a priest to teach you the sutras."

O-Toyo wished it, and asked that an extremely small nun's dress be got for her. But the mother said:—

"Everything except the dress a good nun may have made small. But she must wear a large dress—that is the law of Buddha."

So she was persuaded to wear the same dress as other nuns.

IV

They built for her a small An-dera, or Nun's-Temple, in an empty court where another and larger temple, called Amida-ji, had once stood. The An-dera was also called Amida-ji, and was dedicated to

Amida-Nyorai and to other Buddhas. It was fitted up with a very small altar and with miniature altar furniture. There was a tiny copy of the sutras on a tiny reading-desk, and tiny screens and bells and kakemono. And she dwelt there long after her parents had passed away. People called her the Amida-ji no Bikuni,—which means The Nun of the Temple of Amida.

A little outside the gate there was a statue of Jizo. This Jizo was a special Jizo,—the friend of sick children. There were nearly always offerings of small rice-cakes to be seen before him. These signified that some sick child was being prayed for; and the number of rice-cakes signified the number of the years of the child. Most often there were but two or three cakes; rarely there were seven or ten. The Amida-ji no Bikuni took care of the statue, and supplied it with incense-offerings, and flowers from the temple garden; for there was a small garden behind the An-dera.

After making her morning rounds with the alms-bowl, she would usually seat herself before a very small loom, to weave cloth much too narrow for serious use. But her webs were bought always by certain shopkeepers who knew her story; and they made her presents of very small cups, tiny flower-vases, and queer dwarf-trees for her garden.

Her greatest pleasure was the companionship of children; and this she never lacked. Japanese child-life is mostly passed in temple courts; and many happy childhoods were spent in the court of the Amida-ji. All the mothers in that street liked to have their little ones play there, but cautioned them never to laugh at the Bikuni-San. "Sometimes her ways are strange," they would say; "but that is because she once had a little son, who died, and the pain became too great for her mother's heart. So you must be very good and respectful to her."

Good they were, but not quite respectful in the reverential sense. They knew better than to be that. They called her "Bikuni-San" always, and saluted her nicely; but otherwise they treated her like one of themselves. They played games with her; and she gave them tea in extremely small cups, and made for them heaps of rice-cakes not much bigger than peas, and wove upon her loom cloth of cotton and cloth of silk for the robes of their dolls. So she became to them as a blood-sister.

They played with her daily till they grew too big to play, and left the court of the temple of Amida to begin the bitter work of life, and to become the fathers and mothers of children whom they sent to play in their stead. These learned to love the Bikuni-San like their parents had done. And the Bikuni-San lived to play with the children of the children of the children of those who remembered when her temple was built.

The people took good heed that she should not know want. There was always given to her more than she needed for herself. So she was able to be nearly as kind to the children as she wished, and to feed extravagantly certain small animals. Birds nested in her temple, and ate from her hand, and learned not to perch upon the heads of the Buddhas.

Some days after her funeral, a crowd of children visited my house. A little girl of nine years spoke for them all:—

"Sir, we are asking for the sake of the Bikuni-San who is dead. A very large haka[1] has been set up for her. It is a nice haka. But we want to give her also a very, very small haka, because in the time she was with us she often said she would like a very little haka. And the stone-cutter has promised to cut it for us, and to make it very pretty, if we can bring the money. Therefore perhaps you will honorably give something."

"Assuredly," I said. "But now you will have nowhere to play."

She answered, smiling:—

"We shall still play in the court of the temple of Amida. She is buried there and she will hear our playing, and be glad."

---

1. Tombstone.

IN THE TWILIGHT OF THE GODS

"Do you know anything about josses?"

"Josses?"

"Yes; idols, Japanese idols,—josses."

"Something," I answered, "but not very much."

"Well, come and look at my collection, won't you?
I've been collecting josses for tweny years, and I've
got some worth seeing. They are not for sale, though,
—except to the British Museum."

I followed the curio dealer through the bric-a-brac
of his shop, and across a paved yard into an unusual-
ly large go-down.[1] Like all go-downs it was dark:
I could barely discern a stairway sloping up through
gloom. He paused at the foot.

"You'll be able to see better in a moment," he
said. "I had this place built expressly for them; but
now it is scarcely big enough. They're all in the second story. Go right up; only be careful,—the steps
are bad."

I climbed, and reached a sort of gloaming, under
a very high roof, and found myself face to face with
the gods.

In the dusk of the great go-down the spectacle
was more than weird: it was apparitional. Arhats
and Buddhas and Bodhissatvas, and the shapes of a
mythology older than they, filled all the shadowy
space; not ranked by heirarchies, as in a temple, but
mingled without order, as in a silent panic. Out of
the wilderness of multiple heads and broken aureoles

---

1. A name given to fireproof storehouses in the open ports of the
Far East. The word is derived from the Malay *gadong*.

and hands uplifted in menace or in prayer,—a shimmering confusion of dusty gold half lighted by cobwebbed air-holes in the heavy walls,—I could at first discern little; then, as the dimness cleared, I began to distinguish personalities. I saw Kwannon, of many forms; Jizo, of many names; Shaka, Yakushi, Amida, the Buddhas and their disciples. They were very old; and their art was not all of Japan, nor of any one place or time: there were shapes from Korea, China, India,—treasures brought over sea in the rich days of the early Buddhist missions. Some were seated upon lotos-flowers, the lotos-flowers of the Apparitional Birth. Some rode leopards, tigers, lions, or monsters mystical,—typifying lightning, typifying death. One, triple-headed and many-handed, sinister and splendid, seemed moving through the gloom on a throne of gold, uplifted by a phalanx of elephants. Fudo I saw, shrouded and shrined in fire, and Maya-Fujin, riding her celestial peacock; and strangely mingling with these Buddhist visions, as in the anachronism of a Limbo, armored effigies of daimyo and images of the Chinese sages. There were huge forms of wrath, grasping thunderbolts, and rising to the roof: the Deva-kings, like impersonations of hurricane power; the Ni-O, guardians of long-vanished temple gates. Also there were forms voluptuously feminine: the light grace of the limbs folded within their lotos-cups, the suppleness of the fingers numbering the numbers of the Good Law, were ideals possibly inspired in some forgotten time by the charm of an Indian dancing-girl. Shelved against the naked brickwork above, I could perceive multitudes of lesser shapes: demon figures with eyes that burned through the dark like the eyes of a black cat, and figures half man, half bird, winged and beaked like eagles,—the *Tengu* of Japanese fancy.

"Well?" queried the curio dealer, with a chuckle of satisfaction at my evident surprise.

"It is a very good collection," I responded.

He clapped his hand on my shoulder, and exclaimed triumphantly in my ear, "Cost me fifty thousand dollars."

But the images themselves told me how much more was their cost of forgotten piety, notwithstanding the cheapness of artistic labor in the East. Also they told me of the dead millions whose pilgrim feet had worn hollow the steps leading to their shrines, of the buried mothers who used to suspend little baby-dresses before their altars, of the generations of children taught to murmur prayers to them, of the countless sorrows and hopes confided to them. Ghosts of the worship of centuries had followed them into exile; a thin, sweet odor of incense haunted the dusty place.

"What would you call that?" asked the voice of the curio dealer. "I've been told it's the best of the lot."

He pointed to a figure resting upon a triple golden lotos,—Avalokitesvara: she "who looketh down above the sound of prayer.". . . *Storms and hate give way to her name. Fire is quenched by her name. Demons vanish at the sound of her name. By her name one may stand firm in the sky, like a sun. . . .* The delicacy of the limbs, the tenderness of the smile, were dreams of the Indian paradise.

"It is a Kwannon," I made reply, "and very beautiful."

"Somebody will have to pay me a very beautiful price for it," he said, with a shrewd wink. "It cost me enough! As a rule, though, I get these things very cheap. There are few people who care to buy them, and they have to be sold privately, you know: that gives me an advantage. See that joss in the corner,—the big black fellow? What is it?"

"Emmei-Jizo," I answered,—"Jizo, the giver of long life. It must be very old."

"Well," he said, again taking me by the shoulder, "the man from whom I got that piece was put in prison for selling it to me."

Then he burst into a hearty laugh,—whether at the recollection of his own cleverness in the transaction, or at the unfortunate simplicity of the person who had sold the statue contrary to law, I could not decide.

"Afterwards," he resumed, "they wanted to get it back again, and offered me more than I had given for it. But I held on. I don't know everything about josses, but I do know what they are worth. There isn't another idol like that in the whole country. The British Museum will be glad to get it."

"When do you intend to offer the collection to the British Museum?" I presumed to ask.

"Well, I first want to get up a show," he replied. "There's money to be made by a show of josses in London. London people never saw anything like this in their lives. Then the church folks help that sort of a show, if you manage them properly: it advertises

the missions. 'Heathen idols from Japan!' . . . How
do you like the baby?"

I was looking at a small gold-colored image of a
naked child, standing, one tiny hand pointing up-
ward, and the other downward,—representing the
Buddha newly born. *Sparkling with light he came
from the womb, as when the sun first rises in the
east. . . . Upright he took deliberately seven steps;
and the prints of his feet upon the ground remained
burning as seven stars. And he spake with clearest
utterance, saying, "This birth is a Buddha birth. Re-
birth is not for me. Only this last time am I born for
the salvation of all on earth and in heaven."*

"That is what they call a Tanjo-Shaka," I said.
"It looks like bronze."

"Bronze it is," he responded, tapping it with his
knuckles to make the metal ring. "The bronze alone
is worth more than the price I paid."

I looked at the four Devas whose heads almost
touched the roof, and thought of the story of their
apparition told in the Mahavagga. *On a beautiful
night the Four Great Kings entered the holy grove,
filling all the place with light; and having respectfully
saluted the Blesesd One, they stood in the four di-
rections, like four great firebrands.*

"How did you ever manage to get those big figures
upstairs?" I asked.

"Oh, hauled them up! We've got a hatchway. The
real trouble was getting them here by train. It was
the first railroad trip they ever made. . . . But look at
these here: *they* will make the sensation of the show!"

I looked, and saw two small wooden images, about three feet high.

"Why do you think they will make a sensation?" I inquired innocently.

"Don't you see what they are? They date from the time of the persecutions. *Japanese devils trampling on the Cross!*"

They were small temple guardians only; but their feet rested upon X-shaped supports.

"Did any person tell you these were devils trampling on the Cross?" I made bold to ask.

"What else are they doing?" he answered evasively. "Look at the crosses under their feet!"

"But they are not devils," I insisted; "and those cross-pieces were put under their feet simply to give equilibrium."

He said nothing, but looked disappointed; and I felt a little sorry for him. *Devils trampling on the Cross,* as a display line in some London poster announcing the arrival of "josses from Japan," might certainly have been relied on to catch the public eye.

"This is more wonderful," I said, pointing to a beautiful group,—Maya with the infant Buddha issuing from her side, according to tradition. *Painlessly the Bodhisattva was born from her right side. It was the eighth day of the fourth moon.*

"That's bronze, too," he remarked, tapping it. "Bronze josses are getting rare. We used to buy them up and sell them for old metal. Wish I'd kept some of them! You ought to have seen the bronzes, in those days, coming in from the temples,—bells and vases and josses! That was the time we tried to buy the Daibutsu at Kamakura."

"For old bronze?" I queried.

"Yes. We calculated the weight of the metal, and formed a syndicate. Our first offer was thirty thousand. We could have made a big profit, for there's a good deal of gold and silver in that work. The priests wanted to sell, but the people wouldn't let them."

"It's one of the world's wonders," I said. "Would you really have broken it up?"

"Certainly. Why not? What else could you do with it? . . . That one there looks just like a Virgin Mary, doesn't it?"

He pointed to the gilded image of a female clasping a child to her breast.

"Yes," I replied; "but it is Kishibojin, the goddess who loves little children."

"People talk about idolatry," he went on musingly. "I've seen things like many of these in Roman Catholic chapels. Seems to me religion is pretty much the same the world over."

"I think you are right," I said.

"Why, the story of Buddha is like the story of Christ, isn't it?"

"To some degree," I assented.

"Only, he wasn't crucified."

I did not answer; thinking of the text, *In all the world there is not one spot even so large as a mustard seed where he has not surrendered his body for the sake of creatures.* Then it suddenly seemed to me that this was absolutely true. For the Buddha of the deeper Buddhism is not Gautama, nor yet any one Tathagata, but simply the divine in man. Chrysalids of the infinite we all are: each contains a ghostly Buddha, and the millions are but one. All humanity is potentially the Buddha-to-come, dreaming through the ages in Illusion; and the teacher's smile will make beautiful the world again when selfishness shall die. Every noble sacrifice brings nearer the hour of his awakening; and who may justly doubt—remembering the myriads of the centuries of man—that even now there does not remain one place on earth where life has not been freely given for love or duty?

I felt the curio dealer's hand on my shoulder again.

"At all events," he cried in a cheery tone, "they'll be appreciated in the British Museum—eh?"

"I hope so. They ought to be."

Then I fancied them immured somewhere in that vast necropolis of dead gods, under the gloom of a pea-soup-fog, chambered with forgotten dignities of Egypt or Babylon, and trembling faintly at the roar of London,—all to what end? Perhaps to aid another Alma Tadema to paint the beauty of another vanished civilization; perhaps to assist the illustration of an English Dictionary of Buddhism; perhaps to inspire some future laureate with a metaphor startling as Tennyson's figure of the "oiled and curled Assyrian bull." Assuredly they would not be preserved in vain. The thinkers of a less conventional and selfish era would teach new reverence for them. Each eidolon shaped by human faith remains the shell of a truth eternally divine; and even the shell itself may hold a ghostly power. The soft serenity, the passionless tenderness, of these Buddha faces might yet give peace of soul to a West weary of creeds transformed into conventions, eager for the coming of another teacher to proclaim, *"I have the same feeling for the high as for the low, for the moral as for the immoral, for the depraved as for the virtuous, for those holding sectarian views and false opinions as for those whose beliefs are good and true."*

OTOKICHI'S DARUMA

The young folks are delighted, because last night a heavy fall of snow made for us what the Japanese poets so prettily call "a silver world." . . . Really these poets have been guilty of no extravagance in their charming praises of winter. For in Japan winter is beautiful,—fantastically beautiful. It bestirs no melancholy imaginings about "the death of nature," —inasmuch as nature remains most visibly alive during even the Period of Greatest Cold. It does not afflict the aesthetic eye with the spectacle of "skeleton-woods,"—for the woods largely consist of evergreens. And the snow,—heaping softly upon the needles of the pines, or forcing the bamboos to display their bending grace under its momentary weight, —never suggests to Far-Eastern poet the dismal fancy of a winding-sheet. Indeed the singular charm of Japanese winter is made by this snow,—lumping itself into grotesqueries unimaginable above the constant verdure of woods and gardens.

This morning my two students, Aki and Niimi, have been amusing themselves and the children by making a Yuki-Daruma; and I have been amusing myself by watching them. The rules for making a Yuki-Daruma are ancient and simple. You first compose a huge snowball,—between three and four feet in diameter, if possible,—which is to represent the squatting body of Daruma. Then you make a smaller snowball, about two feet in diameter, to rep-

resent his head; and you put this smaller ball on top
of the other,—packing snow around the under-parts
of both, so as to fix them in place. Two round
lumps of charcoal serve to make eyes for Daruma;
and some irregular fragments of the same material
will suffice to indicate his nose and mouth. Finally,
you must scoop out a hollow in the great belly of
him, to represent a navel, and stick a lighted candle
inside. The warmth of the candle gradually enlarges
the opening. . . .

But I forgot to explain the term Yuki-Daruma, or
Snow-Daruma. "Daruma" is an abbreviation of the
name Bodai-Daruma,—Japanese rendering of the
Sanscrit "Bodhidharma." And who was Bodhidharma?

Bodhidharma or Bodhitara, was the twenty-eighth
patriarch of Buddhism, by succession from the great
Kasyapa. He went to China as a Buddhist missionary
in the first year of the Ryo dynasty (520 A. D.); and
in China he founded the great Zen *(Dhyana)* sect,—
whose doctrine is called "The Doctrine of Thought
transmitted by Thought": that is to say, transmitted
without words, either written or spoken. Says Professor Bunyiu Nanjio, in his *History of the Twelve
Buddhist Sects:*—"Besides all the doctrines of the
Mahayana and Hinayana, there is one distinct line of
transmission of a secret doctrine, which is not subject
to any utterance at all. According to this doctrine,
one is to see the so-called key to the thought of
Buddha, or the nature of Buddha, directly by his own
thought." The tradition of the Zen doctrine is
curious. When the Buddha was preaching upon the

Vulture Peak, there suddenly appeared before him the great Brahma, who presented a gold-colored flower to the Blessed One, and therewith besought him to preach the Law. The Blessed One accepted the heavenly flower, and held it in his hand, but spoke no word. Then the great assembly wondered at the silence of the Blessed One. But the venerable Kasyapa smiled. And the Blessed One said to the venerable Kasyapa:—"I have the wonderful thought of Nirvana, the Eye of the True Law, which I now shall give you." . . . So by thought alone the doctrine was transmitted to Kasyapa; and by thought alone Kasyapa transmitted it to Ananda; and thereafter by thought alone it was transmitted from patriarch to patriarch even to the time of Bodhidharma, who communicated it to his successor, the second Chinese patriarch of the sect. By some writers it is said that Bodhidharma visited Japan; but this statement appears to have little foundation. At all events, the Zen doctrine was not introduced into Japan before the eighth century.

Now of the many legends about Daruma, the most famous is the story that he once remained for nine years in uninterrupted meditation, during which time his legs fell off. Wherefore images of him are made without legs.

Certainly Daruma has large claims to respect. But the artists and the toymakers of the Far East have never allowed these claims to interfere with the indulgence of their sense of humor,—originally bestirred, no doubt, by the story of the loss of his legs. For centuries this legendary mishap has been made the subject of comical drawings and comical carvings; and generations of Japanese children have amused themselves with a certain toy-image of Daruma so contrived that, however the little figure be thrown down, it will always bob up again into a squatting posture. This still popular toy, called *Okiagari-Koboshi* ("The Getting-up Little Priest") may have been originally modelled, or remodelled, after a Chinese toy made upon the same principle, and called *Puh-Tau-Ung* ("The Not-falling-down Old Man"). Mention is made of the *Okiagari-Koboshi* in a Japanese play called *Manju-Kui*, known to have been composed in the fourteenth century. But the earlier forms of the toy do not seem to have been representations of Daruma. There is, however, a children's-song, dating from the seventeenth century, which proves that the Daruma-toy was popular more than two hundred years ago:—

Hi ni! fu ni!
Fundan Daruma ga
Akai zukin kaburi sunmaita!
("Once! twice! . . . Ever the red-hooded Daruma heedlessly sits up again!")

From this little song it would seem that the form of the toy has not been changed since the seventeenth century; Daruma still wears his hood, and is still painted red—all of him except his face.

Besides the Snow-Daruma already described, and the toy-Daruma (usually made of papier-mache), there are countless comical varieties of Daruma: figures moulded or carved in almost every kind of

material, and ranging in size from the tiny metal
Daruma, half-an-inch long, designed for a pouch
clasp, to the big wooden Daruma, two or three feet
high, which the Japanese tobacconist has adopted for
a shop-sign. . . . Thus profanely does popular art
deride the holy legend of the nine years' meditation.

II

Now that Yuki-Daruma in my garden reminds me
of a very peculiar Daruma which I discovered several
years ago, at a certain fishing-village on the eastern
coast where I passed a happy summer. There was
no hotel in the place; but a good man called Otokichi,
who kept a fish-shop, used to let me occupy the upper
part of his house, and fed me with fish cooked in a
wonderful variety of ways.

One morning he called me into his shop to show
me a very fine *hobo*. . . . I wonder if you ever saw
anything resembling a hobo. It looks so much like
a gigantic butterfly or moth, that you must examine
it closely to make sure that it is not an insect, but a
fish,—a sort of gurnard. It has four fins arranged like
pairs of wings,—the upper pair dark, with bright
spots of sky-blue; the lower pair deep red. It seems
also to have legs like a butterfly,—slender legs upon
which it runs about quickly. . . .

"Is it good to eat?" I asked.

"He!" answered Otokichi:—"this shall be prepared for the Honorable Dinner."

(To any question asked of him,—even a question
requiring answer in the negative,—Otokichi would
begin his reply with the exclamation *He* ("Yes"),—

uttered in such a tone of sympathy and good-will as to make the hearer immediately forget all the tribulations of existence.)

Then I wandered back into the shop, looking at things. On one side were rows of shelves supporting boxes of dried fish, and packages of edible seaweed, and bundles of straw sandals, and gourds for holding sake, and bottles of lemonade! On the opposite side, high up, I perceived the *kamidana,*—the Shelf of the Gods; and I noticed, under the *kamidana,* a smaller shelf occupied by a red image of Daruma. Evidently the image was not a toy: there were offerings in front of it. I was not surprised to find Daruma accepted as a household divinity,—because I knew that in many parts of Japan prayers were addressed to him on behalf of children attacked by smallpox. But I was rather startled by the peculiar aspect of Otokichi's Daruma, which had only one eye,—a large and formidable eye that seemed to glare through the dusk of the shop like the eye of a great owl. It was the right eye, and was made of glazed paper. The socket of the left eye was a white void.

Therefore I called to Otokichi:—

"Otokichi San!—did the children knock out the left eye of Daruma Sama?"

"He, he!" sympathetically chuckled Otokichi,— lifting a superb *katsuo* to the cutting-bench,—"he never had a left eye."

"Was he made that way?" I asked.

"He!" responded Otokichi,—as he swept his long knife soundlessly through the argent body,—"the folk here make only blind Darumas. When I got

that Daruma, he had no eyes at all. I made the right eye for him last year,—after a day of great fishing."

"But why not have given him both eyes?" I queried;—"he looks so unhappy with only one eye!"

"He, he!" replied Otokichi,—skillfully ranging the slices of pink-and-silver flesh upon a little mat of glass rods,—"when we have another day of great good fortune, then he shall be given the other eye."

Then I walked about the streets of the village, peeping into the houses and shops; and I discovered various other Darumas in different stages of development,—some without eyes, some with only one, and some with two. I remembered that in Izumo it was especially Hotei,—the big-bellied God of Comfort,—who used to be practically rewarded for his favors. As soon as the worshipper found reason for gratitude, Hotei's recumbent image was put upon a small cushion; and for each additional grace bestowed the god would be given an additional cushion. But it occurred to me that Daruma could not be given more than two eyes: three would change him into the sort of goblin called *Mitsume-Kozo.* . . . I learned, upon inquiry, that when a Daruma has been presented with a pair of eyes, and with sundry small offerings, he is put away to make room for an eyeless successor. The blind Daruma can be expected to do wonderful things, because he has to work for his eyes.

There are many such funny little deities in Japan, —so many that it would need a very big book to describe them; and I have found that the people who worship these queer little gods are, for the most part, pathetically honest. Indeed my own experience would almost justify the belief that the more artless the god, the more honest the man,—though I do not want my reader to make any hasty deductions. I do not wish to imply, for example, that the superlative point of honesty might begin at the vanishing point of the god. Only this much I would venture:—Faith in very small gods,—toy-gods,—belongs to that simplicity of heart which, in this wicked world, makes the nearest possible approach to pure goodness.

On the evening before I left the village, Otokichi brought me his bill,—representing the cost of two months' good cheer;—and the amount proved to be unreasonably small. Of course a present was expected, according to the kindly Japanese custom; but, even taking that fact into consideration, the bill was absurdly honest. The least that I could do to show my appreciation of many things was to double the payment requested; and Otokichi's satisfaction, because perfectly natural and at the same time properly dignified, was something beautiful to see.

I was up and dressed by half-past three the next morning, in order to take an early express-train; but even at that ghostly hour I found a warm breakfast awaiting me downstairs, and Otokichi's little brown daughter ready to serve me. . . . As I swallowed the final bowl of warm tea, my gaze involuntarily wandered in the direction of the household gods, whose tiny lamps were still glowing. Then I noticed that a light was burning also in front of Daruma; and almost in the same instant I perceived that Daruma was looking straight at me—WITH TWO EYES! . . .

KUSA-HIBARI

His cage is exactly two Japanese inches high and one inch and a half wide: its tiny wooden door, turning upon a pivot, will scarcely admit the tip of my little finger. But he has plenty of room in that cage, —room to walk, and jump, and fly; for he is so small that you must look very carefully through the brown-gauze side of it in order to catch a glimpse of him. I have always to turn the cage round and round, several times, in a good light, before I can discover his whereabouts; and then I usually find him resting in one of the upper corners,—clinging, upside down, to his ceiling of gauze.

Imagine a cricket about the size of an ordinary mosquito,—with a pair of antennae much longer than his own body, and so fine that you can only distinguish them against the light. Kusa-Hibari, or "Grass-Lark," is the Japanese name of him; and he is worth in the market exactly twelve cents: that is to say, very much more than his weight in gold. Twelve cents for such a gnat-like thing! . . .

By day he sleeps or meditates, except while occupied with the slice of fresh egg-plant or cucumber which must be poked into his cage every morning. . . . To keep him clean and well fed is somewhat troublesome: could you see him, you would think it absurd to take any pains for the sake of a creature so ridiculously small.

But always at sunset the infinitesimal soul of him awakens: then the room begins to fill with a delicate

and ghostly music of indescribable sweetness,—a
thin, thin silvery rippling and trilling as of tiniest
electric bells. As the darkness deepens, the sound becomes sweeter,—sometimes swelling till the whole
house seems to vibrate with the elfish resonance,—
sometimes thinning down into the faintest imaginable
thread of a voice. But loud or low, it keeps a
penetrating quality that is weird. . . . All night the
atomy thus sings: he ceases only when the temple
bell proclaims the hour of dawn.

Now this tiny song is a song of love,—vague love
of the unseen and unknown. It is quite impossible
that he should ever have seen or known, in this
present existence of his. Not even his ancestors, for
many generations back, could have known anything
of the night-life of the fields, or the amorous value
of song. They were born of eggs hatched in a jar of
clay, in the shop of some insect-merchant; and they
dwelt thereafter only in cages. But he sings the song
of his race as it was sung a myriad years ago, and
as faultlessly as if he understood the exact significance of every note. Of course he did not learn the
song. It is a song of organic memory,—deep, dim
memory of other quintillions of lives, when the ghost
of him shrilled at night from the dewy grasses
of the hills. Then that song brought him love—and
death. He has forgotten all about death; but he re-
members the love. And therefore he sings now—for
the bride that will never come.

So that his longing is unconsciously retrospective:
he cries to the dust of the past,—he calls to the
silence and the gods for the return of time. . . .

Human lovers do very much the same thing without knowing it. They call their illusions an Ideal; and their Ideal is, after all, a mere shadowing of race-experience, a phantom of organic memory. The living present has very little to do with it. . . . Perhaps this atomy also has an ideal, or at least the rudiment of an ideal; but, in any event, the tiny desire must utter its plaint in vain.

The fault is not altogether mine. I had been warned that if the creature were mated, he would cease to sing and would speedily die. But, night after night, the plaintive, sweet, unanswered trilling touched me like a reproach,—became at last an obsession, an affliction, a torment of conscience; and I tried to buy a female. It was too late in the season; there were no more *kusa-hibari* for sale,—either males or females. The insect-merchant laughed and said, "He ought to have died about the twentieth day of the ninth month." (It was already the second day of the tenth month.) But the insect-merchant did not know that I have a good stove in my study, and keep the temperature at above 75°F. Wherefore my grass-lark still sings at the close of the eleventh month, and I hope to keep him alive until the Period of Greatest Cold. However, the rest of his generation are probably dead: neither for love nor money could I now find him a mate. And were I to set him free in order that he might make the search for himself, he could not possible live through a single night, even if fortunate enough to escape by day the multitude of his natural enemies in the garden,—ants, centipedes, and ghastly earth-spiders.

Last evening—the twenty-ninth of the eleventh month—an odd feeling came to me as I sat at my desk: a sense of emptiness in the room. Then I became aware that my grass-lark was silent, contrary to his wont. I went to the silent cage, and found him lying dead beside a dried-up lump of egg-plant as gray and hard as a stone. Evidently he had not been fed for three or four days; but only the night before his death he had been singing wonderfully,—so that I foolishly imagined him to be more than usually contented. My student, Aki, who loves insects, used to feed him; but Aki had gone into the country for a week's holiday, and the duty of caring for the grass-lark had devolved upon Hana, the housemaid. She is not sympathetic, Hana the housemaid. She says that she did not forget the mite,—but there was no more egg-plant. And she had never thought of substituting a slice of onion or of cucumber! . . . I spoke words of reproof to Hana the housemaid, and she dutifully expressed contrition. But the fairy-music has stopped; and the stillness reproaches; and the room is cold, in spite of the stove.

Absurd! . . . I have made a good girl unhappy because of an insect half the size of a barley-grain! The quenching of that infinitesimal life troubles me more than I could have believed possible. . . . Of course, the mere habit of thinking about a creature's wants— even the wants of a cricket—may create, by insensible degrees, an imaginative interest, an attachment of which one becomes conscious only when the relation is broken. Besides, I had felt so much, in the hush of the night, the charm of the delicate voice,—telling of one minute existence dependent upon my will and selfish pleasure, as upon the favor of a god,—telling me also that the atom of ghost in the tiny cage, and the atom of ghost within myself, were forever but one and the same in the deeps of the Vast of being. . . . And then to think of the little creature hungering and thirsting, night after night, and day after day, while the thoughts of his guardian deity were turned to the weaving of dreams! . . . How bravely, nevertheless, he sang on to the very end,—an atrocious end, for he had eaten his own legs! . . . May the gods forgive us all,—especially Hana the housemaid!

Yet, after all, to devour one's own legs for hunger is not the worst that can happen to a being cursed with the gift of song. There are human crickets who must eat their own hearts in order to sing.

MOSQUITOES

With a view to self-protection I have been reading Dr. Howard's book, "Mosquitoes." I am persecuted by mosquitoes. There are several species in my neighborhood; but only one of them is a serious torment,—a tiny needly thing, all silver-speckled and silver-streaked. The puncture of it is sharp as an electric burn; and the mere hum of it has a lancinating quality of tone which foretells the quality of the pain about to come,—much in the same way that a particular smell suggests a particular taste. I find that this mosquito much resembles the creature which Dr. Howard calls *Stegomyia fasciata*, or *Culex fasciatus:* and that its habits are the same as those of the *Stegomyia*. For example, it is diurnal rather than nocturnal, and becomes most troublesome during the afternoon. And I have discovered that it comes from the Buddhist cemetery,—a very old cemetery,—in the rear of my garden.

Dr. Howard's book declares that, in order to rid a neighborhood of mosquitoes, it is only necessary to pour a little petroleum, or kerosene oil, into the stagnant water where they breed. Once a week the oil should be used, "at the rate of one ounce for every fifteen square feet of water surface, and a proportionate quantity for any less surface." . . . But please to consider the conditions of *my* neighborhood.

I have said that my tormentors come from the Buddhist cemetery. Before nearly every tomb in that old cemetery there is a water-receptacle, or cistern, called *mizutame*. In the majority of cases this *mizutame* is simply an oblong cavity chiselled in the broad pedestal supporting the monument; but before tombs of a costly kind, having no pedestal-tank, a larger separate tank is placed, cut out of a single block of stone, and decorated with a family crest, or with symbolic carvings. In front of a tomb of the humblest class, having no *mizatume,* water is placed in cups or other vessels,—for the dead must have water. Flowers must also be offered to them; and before every tomb you will find a pair of bamboo cups, or other flower-vessels; and these, of course, contain water. There is a well in the cemetery to supply water for the graves. Whenever the tombs are visited by relatives and friends of the dead, fresh water is poured into the tanks and cups. But as an old cemetery of this kind contains thousands of *mizutame,* and tens of thousands of flower-vessels, the water in all of these cannot be renewed every day. It becomes stagnant and populous. The deeper tanks seldom get dry;—the rainfall at Tokyo being heavy enough to keep them partly filled during nine months of the twelve.

Well, it is in these tanks and flower-vessels that mine enemies are born: they rise by millions from the water of the dead;—and, according to the Buddhist doctrine, some of them may be reincarnations of those very dead, condemned by the error of former lives to the condition of *Jiki-ketsu-gaki,* or blood-drinking pretas. . . . Anyhow, the malevolence of the *Culex fasciatus* would justify the suspicion that some wicked soul had been compressed into that wailing speck of a body. . . .

Now, to return to the subject of kerosene-oil, you can exterminate the mosquitoes of any locality by covering with a film of kerosene all stagnant water surfaces therein. The larvae die on rising to breathe; and the adult females perish when they approach the water to launch their raft of eggs. And I read, in Dr. Howard's book, that the actual cost of freeing from mosquitoes one American town of fifty thousand inhabitants, does not exceed three hundred dollars! . . .

I wonder what would be said if the city government of Tokyo—which is aggressively scientific and progressive—were suddenly to command that all water-surfaces in the Buddhist cemeteries should be covered, at regular intervals, with a film of kerosene oil! How could the religion which prohibits the taking of any life—even of invisible life—yield to such a mandate? Would filial piety even dream of consenting to obey such an order? And then to think of the cost, in labor and time, of putting kerosene oil, every seven days, into the millions of *mizutame,* and the tens of millions of bamboo flower-cups, in the Tokyo graveyards! . . . Impossible! To free the city from mosquitoes it would be necessary to demolish the ancient graveyards;—and that would signify the ruin of the Buddhist temples attached to them;—and that would mean the disparition of so many charming gardens, with their lotus-ponds and Sanscrit lettered monuments and humpy bridges and holy groves and weirdly-smiling Buddhas! So the extermination of the *Culex fasciatus* would involve the destruction of the poetry of the ancestral cult,—surely too great a price to pay! . . .

Besides, I should like, when my times comes, to be laid away in some Buddhist graveyard of the ancient kind,—so that my ghostly company should be ancient, caring nothing for the fashions and the changes and the disintegrations of Meiji. That old cemetery behind my garden would be a suitable place. Everything there is beautiful with a beauty of exceeding and startling queerness; each tree and stone has been shaped by some old, old ideal which no longer exists in any living brain; even the shadows are not of this time and sun, but of a world forgotten, that never knew steam or electricty or magnetism or—kerosene oil! Also in the boom of the big bell there is a quaintness of tone which awakens feelings, so strangely far-away from all the nineteenth-century part of me, that the faint blind stirrings of them make me afraid,—deliciously afraid. Never do I hear that billowing peal but I become aware of a striving and a fluttering in the abyssal part of my ghost,—a sensation as of memories struggling to reach the light beyond the obscurations of a million million deaths and births. I hope to remain within hearing of that bell. . . . And, considering the possibility of being doomed to the state of a *Jiki-ketsu-gaki*, I want to have my chance of being reborn in some bamboo flower-cup, or *mizatume*, whence I might issue softly, singing my thin and pungent song, to bite some people that I know.

ACKNOWLEDGMENTS

"The Mirror of Matsuyama", from "At Hakata", in *Out of the East*, Houghton, Mifflin and Co., 1895

"The Story of Mimi-Nashi-Hoichi", in *Kwaidan*, Houghton, Mifflin and Co., 1904

"Jiu-Roku-Zakura", in *Kwaidan*, Houghton, Mifflin and Co., 1904

"Oshidori", in *Kwaidan*, Houghton, Mifflin and Co., 1904

"The Reconciliation", in *Shadowings*, Little, Brown and Co., 1900

"Yuki-Onna", in *Kwaidan*, Houghton, Mifflin and Co., 1904

"Of a Promise Kept", in *A Japanese Miscellany*, Little, Brown and Co., 1901

"The Dream of a Summer Day", in *Out of the East*, Houghton, Mifflin and Co., 1895

"A Conservative", in *Kokoro*, Houghton, Mifflin and Co., 1896

"Some Thoughts about Ancestor - Worship", in *Kokoro*, Houghton, Mifflin and Co., 1896

"The Nun of the Temple of Amida", in *Kokoro*, Houghton, Mifflin and Co., 1896

"In the Twilight of the Gods", in *Kokoro*, Houghton, Mifflin and Co., 1896

"Otokichi's Daruma", in *A Japanese Miscellany*, Little, Brown and Co., 1901

"Kusa-Hibari", in *Kotto*, The Macmillan Co., 1902

"Mosquitoes", in *Kwaidan*, Houghton, Mifflin and Co., 1904

Lafcadio Hearn was born in 1850, in the Ionian Isles, of an Anglo-Irish father and a Greek mother. He spent his boyhood in Ireland and in England. At the age of nineteen he came to the United States, and lived here until 1890, when he went to Japan. He died in 1904, in Tokyo, where he was for some time professor of English literature at the Imperial University.

www.ingramcontent.com/pod-product-compliance
Lightning Source LLC
Chambersburg PA
CBHW052008240626
47153CB00008B/2784